Praise For "The Stage is Yours"

"I love it. Well done. It's a really nice framing for people to rethink how they did their lives. The most significant idea to keep in mind is that we are not the script that other people give us; we write our scripts."

—Stephen M.R. Covey

"Once popular and successful, I could afford anything and go anywhere, but my soul felt unfulfilled. Struggling with feelings of inadequacy, I found myself attached to abusive people who took advantage of my kindness. I believed I didn't deserve love and clung to toxic relationships.

Becoming my own life director, I recognized these patterns and identified my values, deciding who to keep in my life and who to let go of. Attending the workshop was a turning point, as it reminded me of my worth and the importance of self-love. I felt lost between the party lifestyle I led and the person I was discovering—my true self.

Thanks to the workshop, I began the journey of self-discovery, making significant changes like moving out from my parents' house and planning to leave the corporate world. Stepping out of my comfort zone has brought me closer to my purpose, and the courage to do so came from my experiences in the life director workshop.

As I heal and grow, those close to me also find healing or gain the power of acceptance and adjustment. Helping others brings joy to my heart, and learning how to do so effectively has been a blessing. Healing is the most valuable form of assistance one can offer, and I now believe in my abilities and worth. I know I can achieve whatever I set my mind to—I am good enough."

—Jessy Saade

"The six-year-old girl said confidently: "I am a Mermaid"; her Twenty-year-old sister laughed and twisted the truth about the meaning of the word to convince the little girl to record her voice saying: "I am a Skeleton" instead. The little girl felt ashamed because it wasn't the first time she had been humiliated by her whole environment and many times at school. The little girl doubted herself every second of every day.

Hello! I am Hala, the little girl who has turned thirty-six years old now. A few months ago, doubts kept haunting me despite eight years of therapy until I became the director of my life. The staging technique healed my childhood wounds and expanded my self-esteem enormously.

Hallelujah! I am finally following the action plan of the Life Director, and for the first time in my life, I started making sharp decisions that are created through very specific and clear strategies supported by ongoing adjustments. My dream life has finally started happening. My new dream home is getting decorated and blossoming with the scents of natural essential oils. I am harvesting my organic produce while I am embraced with the love of trees. My vocation is a business that helps people become their best on a conscious, mental, and physical level. I am open to love and abundance every single day. I allow fear to visit me just like a baby that asks to learn the lessons of courage and unbreakable strength while having "peace" as my best friend is holding my hand every step of the way."

—Hala Hibri

"Anger, fear, guilt, hurt, sadness—the mixture of emotions I deal with daily. Each one of them takes a home in every joint in my body; they colonize my tissues, cells, and DNA.

On a bright day in April 2023, I received a link telling about the Life Director Workshop. Me, who lived by those emotions on a daily basis would've passed on it, however, my fingers couldn't but apply and enroll. And here I am, telling about my rollercoaster of a journey at the end of this book.

As we hear it all the time, words can never express certain emotions, and that's where I'm falling now. What I went through during the workshop was truly out of this world. I, who thought I knew it all, thought that I had dug all my secret dungeons and cleared all the dust of my past. I had no clue that in only 5 days, my life would take a full 180, to the point of no return.

I learned how to channel and redirect my emotions, how to take them in, feel them, learn from them, shift my perspective towards them, and release them with love.

It's magical. This method is extremely innovative, full of love and passion, very clever, and witty. It is well done to the extent that it can reach into a person's deepest pits, declutter them, and prepare them for a new set of props and people as the person goes on with their life.

—**Georges Rizk**

"I was very tight on time and energy, with numerous deadlines to be met. Furthermore, the title The Life Director felt like an oxymoron, sewing together life and theater, two realms that felt very distant to me. Still, on the day before the workshop, Georges insisted once more that I tag along. And I said yes, not knowing that this tiny yes to a strange five-day workshop facilitated by a singer would become a new major point of no return in my life.

I had done years of therapy and had come a long way in my journey of inner work. I was also studying psychology while training to become a life coach, so I was very well familiar with many of the tools and techniques used in these domains. Yet, The Life Director Coaching Method was so different, powerful, and holistic that it catalyzed greater healing and growth in my life while inviting more peace, intimacy, joy, and sovereignty.

This new paradigm, Life is a Play, changed my attitude toward myself, others, and the world I exist in so magically and wonderfully that it became a true joy to spread it all around me.

I am glad and grateful to be playing a role in this beautiful play called Life.

I am blessed by the presence and support of my beloved backstage crew, my backbone.

I am honored to collaborate and dance with every precious actor Life brings my way.

I am the star of my show. I am my own Life Director.

—**Farah Doumani**

The Stage is Yours

A Motivational Book for Self Love, Growth, Discovering Your True Self, and Manifesting The Best Story of Your Life

Nadine Chammas

AUTHORITY
PUBLISHING

3rd edition 2025.

ISBN (Paperback): 978-1-965480-18-2

ISBN (Hardcover): 978-1-965480-11-3

ISBN (eBook): 978-1-965480-02-1

Authority Publishing

www.authority-publishing.com

Printed in the United States of America.

Contents

Foreword by Stephen M.R. Covey

IN THE DARKEST HALLWAYS of the life theater, we find ourselves in need of guidance. This book is an innovative, captivating, and magical tool that will offer you this guidance whether you find yourself too old or too young, too qualified or too inexperienced, way beyond or way behind. A modality that borrows the principles of storytelling, acting, and directing from the world of Theater, mixes them with real-life experiences and applies them to the world of Life. Along the way, this formula will set you center stage, under the brightest spotlight, where you'll shine like a million stars combined in this marvelous journey that is your life.

"I love it. Well done. It's a really nice framing for people to rethink how they did their lives. The most significant idea to keep in mind is that we are not the script that other people give us; we write our scripts."

—Stephen M.R. Covey

New York Times and #1 Wall Street Journal Bestselling Author

Here, I am dedicating my book to myself!

Writing my book—or, in other words, writing my story—has been a long rollercoaster of emotions.

That story got stuck in one of the chapters of my life and was put on pause until I pressed the play button and watched it happening in parallel with what I have missed and who I became after seven years of pause.

I dedicate this book to my inner child, who pushed me to let it all out.

I dedicate this book to the soul of my late mother, who taught me that freedom is life and pushed me to be on stage, sing, and act, as well as to the soul of my late father, who taught me to be authentic and never settle for unfairness.

I dedicate this book to my husband, who is my best friend, for never giving up on me and my dreams, for my daughter and my son, who gave me the space to just be and loved me for who I am, not what I am.

I dedicate this book to my sisters and brothers, who were my first teachers and role models, and to my friends, who waited with me until I was done with it.

I dedicate this book to my spirit guides and St Agatha, who supported and lifted me when I was about to give up on myself.

I believe that we don't meet people by coincidence but rather that they are meant to cross our paths. During these seven years, many people came into my life and played a role in one of the chapters of my story. Some left, and others stayed. Some came at the right moment when I needed motivation or inspiration, and others were just messengers meant to deliver the message and disappear.

I learned to value the presence of every person I meet and receive what they have for me. I also learned to detach emotionally and keep the good memories and lessons while being grateful for all of these people who helped me continue my story. I dedicate this book also to them.

Finally, I extend my dedication to Emiku, whom I will introduce in the following pages.

The Invitation

SEVEN YEARS AGO, I fell in love with you.

And I'm not using the plural "you" here, no. I am addressing you, the singular individual YOU.

I fell in love with you so much that I committed myself to crafting the most breathtaking gift my hands could ever offer you. I kept sculpting and refining my present with such devotion that I eventually surpassed myself.

The process, all along, was sculpting and refining me.

Today, my gift and I are ready, and here is your VIP ticket to the most intimately entertaining and engaging theatrical performance of my life.

During the show, I will reenact very dear and sometimes vulnerable scenes. After every act, I will share the refined gems I found in them and then pass them on to you.

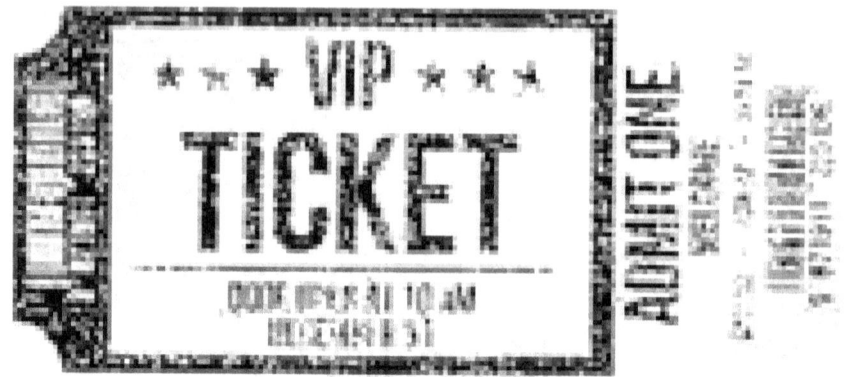

Spoiler: I will show you around the different areas of the theater, too.

These pages are my ultimate gift to you, and your presence would mean the world to me.

Now, just in case you couldn't make it, allow me to utter two words yearning to be heard by you.

Thank **YOU.**

Thank you for being my mirror, my spark, my motive. Thank you for holding me accountable. Thank you for waiting so long. Thank you for turning me into the most breathtaking version of myself.

Yours truly,

Nadine

Prologue

YOU ARE WALKING DOWN a long and dim hallway. The walls are made of luxurious wood panels, and the vibrant red carpet covers the floor. With every step forward, a new thought crosses your mind, making you reconsider the correctness of your decision to come here.

"What does she mean by saying that she fell in love with me seven years ago? Do we know each other? And if she has something to say, why send an invitation? And why this old and empty theater house? I have always walked down this road but never even noticed this theater existed. What type of person would ask to meet up here?"

You take another few steps forward. "This whole thing feels a little weird... a little too weird."

This thought ends as you reach the end of the hallway. A thin, tall, and serious-looking man in a tux stands to the right of a huge, thick wooden door. He remains totally still, as if genuinely uninterested in your arrival.

You take out your ticket and silently hand it over to him.

"You are Emiku," he said with a gentle smile and an amused sparkle in his eyes. He opens the majestic dark brown door, "Please follow me."

"Emiku?" you think to yourself. "There must be some mistake here."

Before having a chance to correct the misunderstanding, you find yourself in an immense old and luxurious theater. Your jaw drops as you contemplate the dazzling balconies, the majestic stage, the velvet seats and curtains... Your usher interrupts your amazement by inviting you with a gracious gesture of his hand to take your seat, the middle seat in the front row, and leaves, gently closing the door behind him like a total professional.

Your attempt to take in all the magic of this place is once again interrupted by the sudden echo of quick yet firm steps clacking against the wooden floor. A charismatic woman with blond hair rushes from behind the curtains at the rear end of the stage onto the middle, captivating your attention.

Bright lights coming from above illuminate her delicate yet vibrant face. Her smile is so wide you could almost feel it stretching beyond her cheeks. Her eyes shimmer with an indescribable excitement and subtle emotion.

"I have been waiting here for you for a long time, Emiku. Your presence is priceless. Thank you."

Introduction

The Life Director

THIS BOOK MAY BE your ultimate guide to restoring your truest self, regaining your greatest sovereignty and reclaiming your fullest life imaginable.

You may feel too old or young, too qualified or inexperienced, way beyond or far behind...

Wherever you think you are, whatever you feel you need, and whoever you believe yourself to be... All these ideas are growing dim now as you contemplate this dazzling fact:

If these words of mine were not yours to read, Emiku, your hands would be holding another book.

"All the world's a stage, and all the men and women merely players"—that's William Shakespeare. I couldn't grasp its meaning until I experienced it fully, for the theater is a representation of life itself.

Theater serves as a platform to explore other perspectives that may go unnoticed. The Theater evokes empathy and deepens our understanding of the human experience by delving into dialogue, monologue, and character portrayal. This is similar in life, where we encounter different positions while perceiving life, which unfolds as a 360-degree panorama.

In the audience, we become observers, loyal to our role as outsiders in life. Backstage, we organize and rest away from the spotlight. Onstage, we play our roles, expressing ourselves, just like in life. This differentiates us between the actor, who detaches to embody the character, and the director, who shapes the play's vision. Hence, sitting in the director's chair offers a full perspective on comprehending life from a broader point of view.

Therefore, in this book, dear Emiku, you will be guided to launch the first Act of your journey as a Life Director.

So, take a deep breath in, sit back, and enjoy the show.

"Who are you? And why are you calling me Emiku?"

I am Nadine Chammas. I am a wife, a mother, a lifelong learner, an educator, a mentor, an inspirational speaker, an author, a singer, a songwriter, and an entrepreneur...

I am also a performing artist, an NLP coach, a transformational counselor, a stage hypnotist, a drama therapist, and a healer... In short, I am a woman passionate about positivity, empowerment, and joy.

I spent most of my life performing on stage and entertaining the masses with my plays and shows. I was the star; the stage was my safe space, lover, and home.

Then, a culmination of pain, grief, and disorientation drove a wedge between us. And I found myself lost in the Theater of Life, rehearsing scripts I didn't write and playing small narratives in which other people starred.

Like a puppet, I was stripped of all my creativity, power, and joy. And when people asked me, "Who are you?" The only answer in my head was, "I have no clue."

But when the consequences of this lifestyle stared me in the eye, I awakened and decided to get my act together. I ditched all the scripts I had adopted and resigned from all the roles I had agreed to perform. I decided to write my own script, embody the protagonist character of my own story, and be the director of my own life.

I am Nadine Chammas, the Life Director.

In this jungle overgrown with tangled masses of confusion, depletion, and powerlessness, I am very fortunate to have found the formula that initiated my dormant self, activated my ultimate sovereignty, and erupted my pending life.

The Life Director is the title I created for myself to represent all that I am, summarize everything I do, and define this formula that totally flipped my life around.

Emiku is the title I created for you, inspired by the Andamanese adjective meaning "direct" and the Japanese meaning meaning "blessed and joyful young spirit." It represents everyone desiring to flip their lives around and become their own Life Director.

Sounds fun, right, Emiku?

"Indeed! But what is this formula about? And what differentiates it from the rest?"

This formula borrows the principles of storytelling, acting, and directing from the world of Theater, mixes them with my life experiences, and applies them to the world of Life.

It could be used as a simple and fun quick fix for skin-deep day-to-day scenarios; it is incredibly effective when time and energy are limited.

It could also be used as a complex and thorough existential exercise, which is exquisitely resourceful when contemplating and reviewing your state of mind and role in life.

This method demands no prerequisites and may further serve as a sweet yet powerful tool to help you assist your child, partner, student, parent, client, and friend on their life journeys.

Because I wanted this method to become well-rooted and memorable to you and your loved ones, I left you my key takeaways in bold and italics at the end of each chapter. Feel free to collect them in your journal or write them down on sticky notes, share them with the people you care for, or rephrase them to your liking, for these tiny vows may grow into potent game-changers if planted and watered well.

"This seems interesting, but it's still a little too ambiguous. Could you tell me some more?"

I love your curiosity and desire for knowledge and control, Emiku. This is how the show will progress.

In Chapter One, I will introduce you to Life as a Play and unravel the domino effect of such a philosophical perspective.

In Chapter Two, I will introduce you to your essence as I share my journey of discovering mine with you. You will meet yourself here as your play's protagonist or main character.

In Chapter Three, I will give you first-hand examples of how to embody your Essence in all the different roles you play in the stages of your life. Here, you will meet yourself as the embodied actor of your play.

In Chapter Four, I will take you on a tour of the stage and the backstage areas of your life's Theater. I will assist you in decluttering your environment and then furnishing it with all the tools and props that you may need for the smooth and effective execution of your theatrical production. Here, you will meet yourself as the stage manager of your play.

In Chapter Five, I will give you a simple and practical tool that will enable you to intentionally define and refine your character and your story development in your next life chapter. Here, you will meet yourself as the scriptwriter of your play.

In Chapter Six, I will share the insights that my life experience taught me about how to discern, dismiss, and recruit the best backstage crew you could ever have. This would be yet another responsibility of yours as a stage manager.

In Chapter Seven, I will help you develop guidelines for discerning, dismissing, and recruiting the best-supporting actors for your play. Here, you will meet yourself as your play's theater director—or life director.

In Chapter Eight, I will support you as you rehearse one last time for your first life show – the embodiment of your refined character before a real live audience. In this final rehearsal, you will stand back and observe your show from the audience's and the life director's perspectives for one final tweak.

In Chapter Nine, I will tell you exactly what you need to do to advertise your show successfully. I will help you select the date and place of your show and the marketing tools and techniques that are most efficient for you. Here, you will meet yourself as the marketing manager of your play.

Finally, in Chapter Ten, I will remind you of all the cues I gave you to live your life as a play and be your life director. I will descend those wooden stairs, sit among the audience, and marvel at you as you take center stage and rock your Life.

Let me go a little bit deeper.

This manuscript you're holding has a twisted layout. As you'll notice later, every chapter starts with a theater script. Each script is a story based on bits and pieces of my life. But remember, a story is just a story. What matters are the feelings it evokes and the morals it leaves engraved.

You'll find two scenes in every act. The first scene describes times in my life when I wasn't in my element, estranged from myself, and very far from my essence. The second scene describes how I handled situations in my life after I had learned all the lessons while asserting myself and embodying my essence.

Each script is preceded by the Dramatis Personae, a page describing the characters in the scene, their physical setting, and the period during which the story takes place.

Every story starts with a "Setting," which describes the stage, the props, and the ambiance. Just below it is "At Rise," a paragraph describing what's happening on stage just as the curtains rise, precisely before the action occurs.

The scripts are very traditional; sometimes, under each character's name, you'll find sentences between parentheses describing how the character reacts, moves, or behaves. The word (Cont.) is repeated many times after a character's name. It indicates that the character will continue speaking after an abrupt stop. The abbreviation (VO) means "Voice Over" and indicates that what's been said is recorded and played alongside the action in the Theater. Then, finally, at the end of every scene, the word "Blackout" appears, signifying that all the lights are off and the scene has reached its end.

Then, after these magical, theatrical, and dramatic journeys, at times too surprising, I expand the Life Director concept. First, you'll find a part where I tell you more about my experience and how it helped me shape my philosophy based on the scenes of that chapter, then a part where I share my philosophy expansively. Finally, you'll reach exercises tailored specifically to help you find answers about yourself.

My hands and heart will celebrate you as you proudly clap for yourself. You've done it, Emiku!

The Life Director method is my life's calling, philosophy, passion, and legacy, and it is my ultimate honor to pass it on to you.

Workbook

I aim to create the world's best method for helping career-driven and goal-oriented individuals sit in The Life Director's chair to connect to their true selves, lead purpose-driven lives, and make an impact. This book is packed full of strategies and tools I used to transform my life and make it my greatest show on earth—the same strategies and tools I use in my life and those I coached.

You can download them all—as a workbook—from www.The LifeDirector.com/Workbook. Click on the link, download the workbook, and get ready to get busy.

Keep your workbook handy and complete it as you read the book.

Chapter One

Life is a Play

Enjoy The Show

MY WHOLE LIFE FLIPPED around when a microscopic shift occurred in my perception of life.

As life evolved from a win-or-lose game into a theatrical play, I evolved from a puppet into the master, from a stunt into the protagonist, and from a supporting actor in other people's plays into the director of my own show.

As my attitude toward life changed, my entire philosophy changed, fine-tuning and reorganizing my values and relationships with myself, others, and the world around me.

Drumroll...

It is my utmost pleasure and honor to present "Life as a Play" to you in this Act, dear Emiku!

"Why play each other... When we can play together?

Why compete... When we can collaborate?"

DRAMATIS PERSONAE

ACT I - SCENE 1

HER - a 20-year-old young singer.

A crowd of couples - they remain silent.

SETTING

In a fine diner.

TIME

Valentine's Eve.

ACT I

SCENE 1

SETTING: Valentine's Eve weaves its enchantment in the warm embrace of a softly lit restaurant. The air is alive with anticipation as crimson roses adorn every table. Couples lean in close, captivated by the promise of an unforgettable evening. Amidst the hushed whispers and stolen glances, the crowd eagerly awaits the singer's debut, ready to be swept away by the melodies that will paint the canvas of their romantic escapade.

AT RISE: Backstage, the singer unzips her black dress; her trembling fingers reveal a vulnerable heart. With each slide of the zipper, a tear escapes her eye, leaving trails of sadness on her powdered cheeks. Reluctantly, she puts on a vibrant red outfit, masking her emotions for the world not to see.

HER

(With a solemn walk, she traverses the stage, tears cascading like a somber symphony for her departed father. Every step becomes an act of sheer will, driven by an unyielding determination. As SHE parts her lips, her desire

3

intensifies, yearning for her employer to grasp the weight of her grief. Yet, as the spotlight engulfs her, her voice trembles, transforming the once-beloved act of singing into a ruthless contractual obligation. For two arduous hours, SHE pours her soul into a performance to an indifferent audience that fails to acknowledge her emotional depths. Duty-bound, SHE persists, determined to fulfill her role)

(BLACKOUT)

(End of Scene 1)

DRAMATIS PERSONAE

ACT I - SCENE 2

HER - a wise young lady, dedicated to herself and her family.

BROTHER - her brother, ten years younger than her, can't face the sudden loss of their mother.

OTHER SIBLINGS- of various age ranges, all sad and desperate, they remain silent throughout the scene.

SETTING

In the cemetery.

TIME

Right after the funeral of her deceased mother. Only ten months after the death of her father.

ACT I

SCENE 2

SETTING: A dismal ambiance envelopes the stage at the solemn gates of the cemetery. It feels like time has been frozen, taking us back to a far-gone era, two decades ago. The skies are ash gray, and the clouds hold the immense weight of memories.

AT RISE: With her back to her mother's tombstone, she stands observing the gates. Among the collective sorrow, her siblings are overwhelmed with tears, letting their emotions flow, waiting for her to leave. Yet, she notices her brother, untouched by tears. She approaches him step by step until she finally reaches his side.

HER

Dear, come near me, for the cuts of loss reach the core of our soul. I understand the pain, yet never burden yourself with restraint.

Burst open the gates of your emotions and allow your tears to run down.

You'll find solace in releasing your anguish; though the scars remain, the burden lessens, and your spirit will be lighter once more.

(SHE hugs him)

BROTHER

(Red-faced, tearing up)

How can this be? She proclaimed she was well a few days ago; it doesn't align! I feel rage, caught in a tempest of sorrow. What will become of me now?

BROTHER (Cont.)

It's like an inferno of questions, torn between the pain of my loss and the burning fury of loneliness and scattering.

HER

(Looks into his eyes, with a tight grip over his shoulders)

Some truths defy our control when they traverse the fabric of existence. Yet, within the depth of sorrow, contemplating her absence, let us find solace in the gentle whisper that she's been liberated from her anguish. Within a shared embrace, my dearest, we find a home in the dance of life's inevitabilities.

(Her brother, unpersuaded, turns around and leaves with his sisters)

(She waits for their silhouettes to dissolve into the distance. Her composure crumbles, the weight of her emotion is insurmountable)

(Lights off, spotlight to her left, herself 10 months ago, is backstage at the restaurant where SHE sings)

PAST SELF

(whimpers, putting on her red dress)

I can't believe that guy; how could he be oblivious to my pleas? Countless times have I told him, I couldn't sing tonight, I'm shattered, Daddy just died, am I not allowed to be weighed down by grief? I vow when our paths cross again, and I'll no longer remain silent, let the world in this wretched restaurant witness my indignation. Defeat is not an option.

(light shines on her in the present again; SHE looks at her enraged past self, but that's not her anymore)

HER

(walks toward her past self, hugs her, and releases her)

This time, I'll do it the right way.

(BLACKOUT)

(End of Act I)

BLACK TO RED

Dearest Emiku. I encountered life's rawness when I lost my parents in such a brief span. I was deeply shocked, and the only thing I could do to cope with that irreversible reality and navigate my swirling emotions was to borrow the tools and techniques from the world of arts and theater and apply them to the real world.

My father passed away on February 2, 2000. And when the owner of the fine diner came to pay his condolences, I realized that he was here to remind me of my performance on Valentine's Eve, that the place was fully booked, and that lovers would be waiting to be entertained.

During that year, I was still a student of fine arts, and little did I know that this education would equip me with valuable tools to confront the challenges I faced during that fateful show on February 13 and the trials that lay ahead. These were the very tools that led me to create the incredible Life Director method that I am sharing with you.

As I unzipped my black dress, I shed off Nadine's grief and clothed myself in the red dress of the singer who owned the stage. Thanks to the actor's tools, I performed flawlessly and captivated the audience amid my deep pain. Yet, when my mother passed away ten months later, performing became an insurmountable challenge. I struggled to disconnect from my sorrow and embody the singer in me. My manager noticed my struggle, and my career as an artist suffered as a result.

I had to step back from the world of performance, for suppress-
ing my negative and raw emotions over time unleashed them to
dominate my inner world and allowed them to hinder my artistic
expression.

My mother's passing away served as an entr'acte, and the key, as
I've come to understand, lies in sublimation, or the redirection and
transformation of the pain and the grief into forms of art. Cooking,
singing, dancing, painting, writing, and other means of creative
expression helped me transform my inner turmoil into something
powerful and meaningful.

A GAME OR A PLAY?

As we grow up, we learn to perceive life as a game with goals, scores,
and competitors. Without a map, we embark toward one destination or another long before we know who we are. Then we struggle
to navigate the waters and weather, weighed down with rusty rules,
overwhelmed with endless expectations, obsessed with perfecting
ourselves, and ashamed to say that we need help or a break. So, we
keep acting strong on the outside while suffering on the inside.

I adopted this attitude toward life, too, Emiku. And I kept pushing
until my tank ran dry and my sails ripped off. Then, in 2014, just
before the shipwreck, disorientation, torment, disarray, deception,

loss, grief, and disease joined forces to recalibrate my compass and illuminate how delicate and transient Life is.

"I already know this about life," you say to yourself.

Well, Emiku, I thought I did, too, especially since I had already suffered the great loss of both my parents by then. However, mumbling this truth with fogged-up thoughts occasionally was not enough. And running away from it and then getting caught up by it at hospitals and funerals was not enough either.

Life as it truly is was inviting me to confront it, make peace with it, and learn how to collaborate with it so that it could heal me, liberate me, and re-birth me into who I truly am.

THE START

I was birthed again on the sandy shore of my homeland, Lebanon. My bruised, stitched, and aching body struggled to stand straight, and I even judged myself totally insane for going there in such weather and at such a time. But like an old sailor enchanted with the melody of the sea, I knew that my long-awaited salvation was calling, and I answered. And as I surrendered, the raging waves crashing at my feet whispered gently to my heart: "Life is a Play, Nadine... Life is a Play."

And zap! These four words snapped me out of my somber slumber, and I stared eyes wide open as the walls of my cave got knocked down, one by one, revealing a dazzling landscape that was always a simple shift of perception away.

EMIKU, MEET LIFE

Now sit comfortably, Emiku, and gaze into the distance for a moment. Imagine yourself standing all alone on a long sandy shore. The wind is strong, and the temperature is cold. You stare at the dark horizon as familiar yet uncomfortable emotions spread below your skin... They may be emotions you are experiencing in the present season of your life, emotions recalled from a recent past, or emotions anticipated in the future. Feelings and thoughts arise, too.

Now, take in one deep breath after the other as you allow these emotions, feelings, and thoughts to engulf you for a minute or two. Then, close your eyes as the words "Life is a Play" echo in your head.

What did the waves tell you?

Tip – The Body
The body is a great medium, storage tank, and gauging tool. Listen to it, for it speaks... all the time.

GLADIATOR OR ACTOR?

In ancient Rome, several types of public games used to be sponsored by the emperor to entertain the wealthy and the bored and divert the attention of the hungry and the miserable. The Roman games included chariot races, animal fights, public executions, and gladiator battles.

After swearing their oath to endure hideous pains, the gladiators were now free in the stadium, fighting like savages with refined skills and sharp tools. The only way a vanquished contestant could win the rare chance to be carried back into his cage alive was to receive the pardon of an insatiable crowd. If the show he put up with his own flesh and bones was not good enough, he was sentenced to death.

To me, Life is not a Roman game anymore, Emiku. Life is a Play.

And ironically, the essence of these four words was not new to me. I tangoed with them many times while majoring in performing arts and practiced their steps countless times as a cherished singer and actress. My medicine was literally hiding in plain sight all along!

Yet, these four words were not a magic spell of some sort, Emiku. Rather, they were a key that finally unlocked for me the great treasure chest of the analogy between Life and Theater. This priceless mystery, infused with the gems of wisdom and skill I collected over the years, gently unfolded the tapestry of my new reality. This new worldview, the Play Worldview, rearranged my Play Values, inspiring my Play Guidelines for living.

A PARADIGM SHIFT

The Play Worldview:

Life is a Play, and the Earth is the theater.

Every human being across history is a unique, original, and indispensable character in the Play of Life.

We succeeded at the auditions and were chosen to play each a very special role that no one else ever could – our unique selves.

During our time here, we are responsible for playing our roles as loyally and outstandingly as possible.

My life is a play, and my environment is my theater.

I am the director of my own play. I am responsible for directing and perfecting my show.

I am the scriptwriter of my story. I am responsible for writing and refining my script.

I am the star of my show. I am responsible for embodying and fine-tuning my character.

The Play Core Values:

Presence

Love

Authenticity

Youthfulness

The Play Guidelines:

I embrace my character, my environment, and others.

I value presence. I accept and collaborate with what is inevitable and uncontrollable, such as the laws of physics, the limits of technology, my height, my parents' pasts, the existence of certain insects, and other people's wounds and desires.

I am thankful for having a role to play in the story of Life. I am grateful for my character, the world I am in, and all others in it. Regardless of who they are and their role, without them, my story is like a carriage without wheels.

I serve my character, my environment, and others.

I value love. I am a positive, responsible, and conscious person. I serve myself by ensuring my own survival, security, empowerment, wellness, sustainability, and fulfillment. I set and respect good physical, mental, and emotional boundaries to protect and love myself.

I coexist with others in harmony and collaboration. And I empower and love the world around me by respecting its boundaries and providing support when possible.

I Revere My Character, My Environment, and Others

I value authenticity. I am unwaveringly loyal to the essence of my character. All characters have beauty and imperfections, and I choose to adhere to my character profile, role, and lines. I naturally and joyfully embody the essence of my character, and I refine my performance every day.

I revere the world around me by acknowledging it for what it is and supporting and enhancing its uniqueness and diversity.

I Arouse My Character, my Environment, and Others

I value youthfulness. I am in love with myself and Life. I am open, curious, and excited about Life. I passionately pursue what sets my heart on fire, and just like children, I incessantly seek new learnings and unfamiliar experiences.

I effortlessly find and plant inspiration around me. I pledge to encourage my entourage and kindle its passions, dreams, and potential. Finally, I reassess and clear old, dysfunctional, and toxic thoughts, objects, and relationships to ensure aliveness, freshness, and vibrancy in my life and the world around me.

I can hear all the sentences swirling together in a raging storm inside your head right now, Emiku. Most of them are either conditional questions starting with "how" or argumentative objections rallying together to refute some of the words I said.

It's okay, Emiku. I've been there, too, and have already weathered this storm before you. If you hang with me here long enough, I'm certain that you will, too.

REVERBERATIONS

Before we move on to Chapter Two, please sit back and relax in your chair again.

Now, close your eyes and focus on your breath. Try to feel your body parts, one by one, starting with the top of your head and ending with the soles of your feet. As you inhale, take in the white freshness of a new breath. And as you exhale, wash out the fumes that are floating in your head. As your mind relaxes, invite the essence of what you just read to fill up your body like a gentle, colorful breeze.

If Life is a Play, what would I appreciate? What would I change?

Tip – Playful Openness

Adopting a child's attitude toward challenges and uncharted territories turns the dreaded hardship into an awaited adventure.

"I am devoted to myself and Life."

Chapter Two

I am All

I am the revealer of the universe

FOR MANY YEARS, PEOPLE knew me as a successful woman.

And despite my uninterrupted gratitude for all my achievements and possessions, I was deeply sad and unfulfilled for being disconnected from myself. I always knew that change was inevitable.

So, when the wisdom of the waves crushed my corroded perception, all the assumptions and implications inspired by it crumbled and were dispelled into the sand, clearing the way for my new Play philosophy to construct my new home for me. And amidst these crazy shifts, nothing else was left but me.

This realization ignited my commitment to discovering myself and building true intimacy with myself. So, I embarked on a treasure hunt to find and retrieve the original pieces of my essence that had become scattered and concealed over the years.

Drumroll...

In this Act, Emiku, it is my utmost pleasure and honor to present to you the revealing of your essence!

"Seasons change, yet I remain."

DRAMATIS PERSONAE

ACT II - SCENE 1

ECHO - the sound of HER mind that she's been yearning to hear for too long.

HER - a bright young lady, brought down a bit by the burdens of her self-discovery and retrieval.

BUSINESSMAN — the character in Antoine de Saint-Exupery's "Little Prince" novel who wanted to own the stars. He represents the epitome of the grownups, appreciating silly logic and forgetting what's beautiful.

LADY TREMAINE - the character in the "Cinderella" tale by the Grimm Brothers. She is the cold-hearted stepmother of Cinderella, representing people who abuse others psychologically, eluding them to the thought that they're unworthy and naïve.

RINGMASTER - the character in the "Dumbo" tale by Helen Aberson-Mayer and Harold Pearl. He plays the role of the unsympathetic showperson who only wants the show to go on to impress the audience.

URSULA - the character in "The Little Mermaid" tale by Hans Christian Andersen. She steals Ariel's voice and abuses her, representing the embodiment of being marginalized and not having a say in one's own life.

SETTING

In the bedroom.

TIME

When she was a young teenager.

ACT II

SCENE 1

SETTING: The sheets are chaotic on a small bed in her bedroom. An alarm clock sits on the bedside table, and a lamp dimly lights the room. To the right, books of old fairytale stories adorn the bookshelf hanging on the wall.

AT RISE: she sits on her bed, legs crossed, humming a gentle tune, rocking back and forth while closing her eyes.

ECHO (VO)

Sweetheart, what's keeping you awake?

HER

(Opens her eyes, startled)

ECHO (VO)

You've been sitting on the bed for too long, and the feelings of despair are undeniable upon this sweet face of yours.

HER

(Closes her eyes, about to cry)

ECHO (VO)

Fear not, for I have a key that might help you out.

(An ornamented antique box falls from above into her arms; a letter is attached to it)

HER

(Reads the letter)

This puzzle is merely a clue...

A proclamation of unity, a phrase to convey,

Once solved, you'll find the words to say.

Unveil the truth, tell yourself, who are you?

(She opens the box; puzzle pieces and small jewels of colors lay dispersed in chaos. She takes them out and starts putting them together following the shades and shapes, for no reference, lays over the box they came in)

(As she puts the last piece of the puzzle, a look of utter satisfaction and hope reigns on her face, while a loud WHOOSH sound rises suddenly, and a man in a suit appears next to her)

HER

(Stutters)

BUSINESSMAN

(The Little Prince)

(An area of the puzzle abruptly, and starts speaking in a slow, dull tone)

Child, you're doing this wrong. This puzzle looks hideous, I might say. It's messy, chaotic, and disgusting. Here you go: Take those pieces and put them in here.

(He points to a certain area in the puzzle)

BUSINESSMAN (cont.)

Those pieces represent logic. Only logic will serve you. You're not about fantasies and dreams; just have logic. You're only bound to be a mathematician; never forget this.

(He exits the room)

(Another WHOOSH sound booms in the room, and an old lady appears, snobbish, in a purple dress)

LADY TREMAINE

(Cinderella)

(Speaks in an accent)

I can't believe this; as soon as I saw this sorcery, I had to come right away.

HER

(Baffled)

LADY TREMAINE

(Smirks, will robbing a handful of pieces from a different area of the final picture)

Aren't you naïve? This puzzle you're putting together is just stupid, considering how blind a girl can be. Take those pieces and place them correctly.

(Giving her a dozen pieces and ushering her to a different area)

LADY TREMAINE (VO)

Those pieces make a picture complete; they represent hard work and sacrifice, that you're a woman, and that you're meant to be only a dedicated wife and mother. Expel the idiocy of living freely. That's just absurd.

(LADY TREMAINE, puts the pieces she took in her purse, as SHE reluctantly struggles to fit the pieces given to her)

HER

(After placing the new pieces, a third whoosh sound comes out, and a big man with a whip enters the room)

RINGMASTER

(Dumbo)

(Speaking in a loud and melodic tone)

Ladies and gentlemen, boys and girls, behold the greatest show of your life.

HER

(Bewildered)

RINGMASTER

(With his long pointy stick, he takes away pieces from a third area of the puzzle)

Forget about what you just put in this puzzle and put those pieces instead.

(Hands her a bunch of pieces that SHE stares at as he proceeds)

RINGMASTER (cont.)

You're only meant to please your crowds. The original pieces you put together earlier don't work for you. Listen carefully, and abide by my words. You're only another elephant on a ball. Give the crowd what they need, even if it costs you sweat and pain.

(He leaves without looking back, as a last WHOOSH sound blurs the room and an eccentric woman dressed in purple and black stomps the wooden floor)

HER

(Wearily gulps)

URSULA

(The Little Mermaid)

You poor soul, what a disturbing picture.

(She robs quickly a whole area of HER picture)

(SHE complies, not having a word to reply)

URSULA

It perplexes me, I must confess, you're still holding on to your youthful spirit; what a shame.

(Utters loudly at HER as she turns around in disbelief, waving her hands in the air)

URSULA

Grow the hell up! Pull yourself together, kid. This children's attitude will lead you absolutely nowhere. Do you want to be loved? Abandon this realm of dreams and fantasies you live in. Emulate the people around you and grow as dim as possible like adults.

(She hands HER new pieces as she storms out of the room)

HER

(Sits still on the bed, looking at the new version of the puzzle in front of her. All the pieces fit, though the image looks very different now)

I want to be a mathematician, and I do believe in logic.

I want to be a wife and mother and believe in sacrifices.

I want to be a performer and believe in entertaining others.

I want to be loved, and I do believe in conformity.

HER

(Sighs heavily)

Then, the answer to the riddle must be...

I'm an amalgamation of disparate patches;

A puzzle constructed by countless hands;

It should satisfy the eyes of its beholders;

Regardless of the original depiction

(BLACKOUT)

(END OF SCENE 1)

DRAMATIS PERSONAE

ACT II - SCENE 2

HER - a young lady, just about to face a turning point in her life.

VOICE - a resonating reverberation that shakes her being and brings her back to her element.

SETTING

On the seashore in Lebanon.

TIME

At a time in her adult life, after going through tough times physically.

ACT II

SCENE 2

SETTING: Under a dimly lit midnight sky, a sandy seashore stretches. Waves crash arrhythmically, reverberating through the air. Above, the moon hangs low, just behind a cluster of dark clouds, reduced to a mere toenail-sized sliver. The wind howls extremely loudly. Huts stand shuttered, and two small boats rest nearby, bound by weathered cords to an embedded nail in the soft sand.

AT RISE: SHE walks on the sandy beach, looking at the horizon. The moon casts a reflection on her face, revealing emotions of sorrow and grief that weigh upon her. The wind whips through her hair, leaving it disheveled. Her long coat flutters and trembles in sync with the heaviness in her heart.

(The wind seizes to blow)

HER

(Bewildered, she stops center stage; she looks around)

(A sweet symphony starts to embrace her surroundings: a violin, a cello, a ukulele, and what seems like some percussion instrument playing a gentle, slow beat. It wasn't an orchestra per se; that was the work of nature, conspiring to bring upon her an encounter that she wasn't expecting)

HER

(Soothed by this sweet, mysterious symphony, she parts her lips, vocalizing with the tune. She recognizes the melody; it's "L'Hymne à l'amour" by Édith Piaf, and for the first time since the death of her mother, she sings)

(The music stops, she's silent, she closes her eyes, and a sweet, gentle voice echoes around her)

VOICE (VO)

You've been missed.

HER

(Gasps and looks around)

Who's there?

VOICE (VO)

(Chuckles)

HER

Where are you?

VOICE (VO)

We're all around you.

We live inside of you.

We're what contains you.

We're in the deepest grooves of your heart.

HER

Why have I been missed, you say?

VOICE (VO)

This voice, this presence, you've been keeping it for yourself for too long, dear.

HER

Silent echoes have replaced my melodies, for it has been ages since I last sang. Even now, when I attempt to let out notes from my lips, they carry searing pain. Ever since my mother departed from this world, it feels as if she carried away the very essence of my voice alongside her own presence.

VOICE (VO)

You have no right to deny yourself the right of expressing this beautiful spirit you have, it's an injustice to withhold such profound treasure that dwells in your being.

HER

No one's willing to listen to me.

VOICE (VO)

What about us? Don't we count?

And what about you? Don't you deserve it?

Sing for us, my dear.

Sing for the sake of the ages of pain you've been through.

Sing for every scar embedded in your soul.

Sing for your mother, your father, and yourself.

Sing for the child in you that's been yearning for this, year after year.

Sing for the bright future ahead of you.

For the joyful moments of perfect presence.

Sing for us—us who engulf and hold and caress you.

Sing for yourself.

Sing as if there are millions of people watching you.

Stand proud of your essence.

And in the end, applaud yourself.

HER

(She takes a deep breath in, lets it out, and opens her eyes, a gentle tear rolls down her cheek, she's been released, she smiles, turns around, and leaves the stage)

(BLACKOUT)

(END OF ACT II)

REAL-LIFE THEATER

As a young girl, I was fascinated by my neighbor, a scientist and artist whose charisma and lifestyle captivated me. Since I excelled in academics at school, I pursued architecture. I enrolled in the same fine arts campus with my sister Zeina, who was studying theater there, and I found myself drawn into the world of creative expression.

Though I never envisioned a career for myself in the performing arts, a pivotal moment changed everything; I entered the university cafeteria and saw my sister bawling her eyes out on the day before her graduation project. She had chosen to present a tough play, "Endgame" by Samuel Becket, and after six months of hard work and endless practice, her main actors abandoned her, leaving her crushed, distraught, and terrified of failure.

Wanting to support her in every way possible, I suggested a daring solution: transform the two male characters into females and perform the roles ourselves the next day. We rehearsed tirelessly all night, and, against all odds, we delivered a spellbinding performance that earned her the highest grade.

I still vividly remember my mother's words, who was still among us at the time: "Your place is here, sweetheart... on the stage. You are born to be here. Please drop out of architecture and join your sister because you two on stage can make miracles together." And thank God I did!

Embracing the art of acting transformed my life and offered profound insights into navigating the complexities of my human existence and finding my true self in the moment.

Acting taught me how to master my own emotions, observe my thoughts in real life, and be present. It taught me how to empty myself and become a clear and clean vessel ready to borrow emotions from the outside to serve my roles. It taught me how to embody one role at a time, avoiding the overwhelming loop we find ourselves in when we try to play multiple personas in our daily lives. And finally, acting taught me the actor's mantra: "I am anywhere, and I am everywhere. I am anyone, and I am everyone. I am the revealer of the universe. I am all."

Isn't this what the spiritual masters teach? "Be still. Be the observer of your thoughts; be present." However, we were never taught how to be actors in real life, which is where my method comes in.

CURIOSITY

During my self-retrieval journey, asking questions was the one super evident yet underrated tool that proved unfailing and efficient in helping me find the answers.

Asking questions is the compass that helped me find my way back home to my essence and continues to ground me in it. Though super simple, this priceless exercise totally changed my life and could amazingly serve you well, too.

When you were a child, probably around the age of two, you began to increasingly ask questions starting with "where," "how," and "why" to make sense of yourself and the world around you and strengthen your sense of security and confidence. Ironically, as years passed by, it is likely that you may have believed that you've got it all figured out or should have, with all the information and experience that you collected. Your decreased curiosity may have pushed you to become duller at asking questions, or it may have caused you to stop asking questions altogether.

If you could sustain and enjoy your childlike curiosity despite the coldness and the criticism, I would like to take a moment to celebrate you and your brave, youthful spirit. How amazing it is to be on this adventure with you, Emiku. Thank you.

However, you may have gotten entangled in the webs of seriousness and pride, mistakenly considered prerequisites to responsibility and adulthood. If so, it's okay, Emiku. I lost myself there for a long time, too, and I hope our playtime together will reignite the curious and explorative child within you.

ANSWERS TO QUESTIONS

Asking questions opens the doors before the answers that are yours to receive. Thus, my loveliest Emiku, I will ask you many questions throughout our rendezvous together to invoke your answers and bring you closer to your essence and calling.

Just as you depend on one tool more than the other to memorize a date or use one language more naturally to express love, similarly, answers come to you in the most understandable forms.

You may hear them as clear words or sentences echoing in your mind. You may see them in the coded symbols of mental images or dreams. Or you may seem to stumble upon them like clues to a treasure hunt scattered in books, random speeches on the web, or our writing. Whichever the form, when an answer comes, you know it... You know you've just been thrown a gem because you already feel wealthier, wiser, calmer... and interestingly, genuinely more curious. When these feelings arise, notice them and record how they move in your body. These are your anchor, your compass, your touchstone.

All of these apply even if you cannot take your time to answer, for merely skimming through the questions is enough a catalyst for the pending chemical reactions that are ready to start.

THE SEED

We humans, as a species, are a part of Nature. Along with other animals and plants, we are a beautiful expression of Life. When we contemplate Nature as if it were a mirror, searching for reflections of us in the environment around us, we form links and parallels that merge into metaphors that artistically simplify and deepen our understanding of our seemingly complex nature.

Fruit trees, in particular, offer a great mirror for the upcoming exercises. Unless they were clones, trees had distinct DNA that separated them from all other trees. This means that they were individually unique, just like us.

While the growth of a fruit tree is influenced by its environment, its unique genetic coding is found in its seed. Thus, in an optimal environment, the tree is the living expression of its seed, and its fruits are its beautiful gift to the world.

You are a fruit tree, and your essence is the seed.

YOUR ESSENCE

Close your eyes, Emiku, and breathe deeply for a few seconds. Deep inhales and slow exhales. Now, connect to your heart. Visualize this organ that is a little bigger than your fist pulsating with life, incessantly pumping a vibrant red freshness to every organ in your body. Surrender to the sensation of aliveness vibrating in your cells. Feel it. Savor it. Now, with a clear and open mind, ask this little yet potent heart of yours, "Who am I?"

Sit in silence and observe.

What did your heart tell and show you?

Tip – Bird's Eye View

Watching your own life from far above can show you things you could never see from within the tornado.

THE BACKSTORY

When people ask, "Who are you?" they usually seek specific information deemed valuable and necessary to fill in the blanks of their template sheet for new acquaintances. Their focus might change from one culture or setting to another. However, their data inquiry usually seems to be occupied with the standard categories we find in census surveys: name, gender, age, nationality, marital status, lineage, level of education, occupation, possessions, etc. And when the collectors are extra curious, courteous, or interested, they might dive into the bonus areas of hobbies, competencies, and achievements. These can be very good and informative, but they are not who we are.

In the world of Theater, such information fills up a few sections of what is known as the character's backstory. A backstory includes all the details from a character's background story relevant to their role in the play. In addition to the information provided by censuses, a backstory may include the major life events of the character, as well as their childhood, main challenges, and overall context. It explains a character's choices, decisions, and attitudes and expands the story.

Without each of your previous versions, you would have never become the amazing person you are today. Thus, the degree to which you love yourself today is a mere reflection of your joyful acceptance of your past and your sense of owning it up. Assuming responsibility for all the experiences you formed makes you their owner, the landlord of the fields who gets to harvest and reap all the beautiful fruits they bring forth.

As such, the backstory is an essential and valuable part of any character's story in a play. It is the backdrop that the scriptwriter uses to highlight the character's strengths and progress in overcoming their weaknesses, surpassing themselves, turning their shame into pride, and turning their failures into powers. Still, a backstory is just a backstory. It does not define nor delimit the character, constituting only one part of a full character profile.

THE CHARACTER PROFILE

When writing a good character profile, a proficient playwright elaborates all they know about the character, giving the actor enough material to answer the question "Who am I?" spontaneously and exhaustively. The more detailed and comprehensive the description is, the greater the odds are to behold an exquisite script, a flawless story, and an outstanding performance – the genuine incarnation of the character.

Thus, a good character profile includes the categories found in census surveys and the character's origins, physical appearance, backstory, and major achievements. But it goes beyond them to encompass everything that fundamentally reflects the character's essence.

We're meant to embody our essence in real life and not create it. Embracing all the facets of its reality. Thus, writing a real-life character profile is about describing the past and not reinventing it. It's about discovering our unique essence and not borrowing bits and pieces from others around us as we pretend to be what we're not.

PEELING THE LAYERS

Paces and rhythms might differ, but in the end, we all change. While the change rate for some of us might be so slow that we appear to have remained the same throughout the years, others make such huge leaps in such short intervals that they might stop identifying with their previous versions. Whether you fall into the first or second category, you are who you are and will always be you, regardless of the changes you might show.

Throughout our lives, we use our experiences to make sense of our identity and to mirror ourselves back to us. So we start "identifying" with the country we're born in, our social status, our political affiliations, the music we listen to, the diet we choose, etc. And along the way, we forget that these external things are mere mirrors and expressions of a deeper existence. So we start confusing who we are with the experiences that we develop, losing track of our essence and becoming estranged from it. However, this situation can always be redeemed, and we can regain sight of our true, unique identity. We need to peel off the layers.

FROM THE SEED DOWN TO THE ROOTS

If your essence is the seed, your birth and coming into existence are your germination. The first step of this process is the downward growth of the main root, which grants the seed access to life. This main root is your childhood, the first era of your essence's backstory.

The many branch roots that grow from it are the life experiences your essence develops along the way. The more numerous the roots and the deeper they go, the bigger and steadier the tree gets.

Asking, "Who am I?" resembles following these roots from their ends to the very base of the main root, which is the closest you could get to your essence, the seed. Thus, the deeper and more diverse your questions stemming from "Who am I?" get, the deeper your digging into your soil of self-knowledge gets, and the deeper your anchoring of "I am" gets.

PIT STOPS AND MILESTONES

Now sit back, Emiku, relax in your chair, and close your eyes. Breathe in, then exhale as deeply as you can, emptying your lungs and belly from all the air in them before inhaling again. Take a deep breath in, then empty yourself again with a strong and deep exhale. Feel your head filling up with oxygen like a balloon filled with Helium. What color is the balloon? Feel your spine stretching up like the thread hanging from this balloon. How long is the thread? You are light.

Imagine your chair turning into a vintage wooden time capsule. Its majestic interior feels familiar, kind, and warm. You are safe. This time capsule came with a purpose. It desires to remind you of what made, shaped, and influenced you. It will show you some important events that helped sculpt you into the stunning piece of art and precious human being you are today.

Take a deeper breath in and feel your courage and gratitude filling you up and elevating the balloon even higher. You are glad and proud to be who you are. Now, feel this time capsule lifting you and taking you on a journey to the past. Your past. Notice its pit stops, their sequence, and their dates. Notice the forms that you take and the emotions that you feel. Notice the people and objects that you see.

What did your vintage time capsule
show you?

Tip – Neutrality

Distancing yourself from your situation and practicing neutrality
is a sure road to learning and growth.

"I am devoted to the unveiling
of my essence."

Chapter Three

Many Lives, Many Roles
All in One Lifetime

FOR A LONG TIME, I believed I had as many identities as the titles and roles I assumed.

However, things changed drastically after my spectacular emancipation at the shores of Lebanon when I realized that, in reality, my essence was one, and I was given the gift of living many lives, as many as the experiences I had. Getting in touch with my essence helped me filter and reprioritize my roles, then fueled my desire and passion to pour my magic into all of them... I became Nadine, the life director, expressing myself in and through the wife and the mother, the actress, and the fundraiser, the coach and the singer, the friend and the entrepreneur. Each one of these roles became a mere incarnation of my one character, just wearing different costumes appropriate to the specific roles that each scene highlights.

Drumroll...

In this Act, my sweet Emiku, it is a true pleasure and a great honor to present the embodiment of your essence to you!

"My costumes are many, yet I am one."

DRAMATIS PERSONAE

ACT III - SCENE 1

HER - a grown lady, feeling miserable, unworthy, and lost.

SETTING

An imaginary stage holding three podiums, each showing parts of her life.

TIME

A scene out of place and time.

ACT III

SCENE 1

SETTING: Three podiums are placed on center stage. Each one is hidden behind a velvet curtain.

AT RISE: A dazzling golden light shines over each podium, emphasizing each one. The rest of the stage remains pitch black.

(The stage becomes obscure, and a gloomy green light shines over the podium to the left. The curtain falls to the ground)

(On the podium, a scene is revealed. SHE is in the middle of nowhere, a mirage of her kids and husband appears. SHE tries to call them. SHE can't. While her family, in the distance, seems to be screaming for her to join them. SHE can't)

HER (VO)

That's the bitter truth.

I should've foreseen this.

I can't take good care of my family.

While I so confidently preach to people.

About positive parenting.

And I'm not even able to apply it myself.

I'm on the verge of a fatal loss.

(The scene on the podium continues in slow motion, where all of a sudden a second green light bursts over the podium to the right and its curtain drops)

(The podium materializes a scene of her in her room. Her hair is a mess, SHE's not dressed well, SHE's deeply shattered)

HER (VO)

I can't handle this anymore.

I don't know who I am.

I'm scared.

I fear telling what I do.

I'm constantly judged.

They're right; who do I take myself for?

I'm not even close to being an inspiration.

Who on earth would be inspired by me?

(As soon as SHE becomes silent, the middle podium
lights up with another green light, and its curtain reaches
the wooden stage)

(Portrayed in this podium is a scene where SHE's on
stage. SHE trips in front of everyone; SHE's not okay.
SHE gets up and starts to perform. SHE forgets the
lyrics. Her dance moves are out of sync. Her mind is
somewhere else)

HER (VO)

I don't want to sing anymore.

My voice crackles.

And I don't want to perform.

I can't even act out my own roles in life.

What kind of artist am I?

What a failure I have become!

I give up; I give all of this up.

My feet shall never touch the stage.

My mouth shall never whisper in a microphone.

I will no longer dance and move.

But what about my life?

What about my kids?

What about my husband?

How did I get here?

I have no clue what to do.

(BLACKOUT)

(END OF SCENE 1)

DRAMATIS PERSONAE

ACT III - SCENE 2

HER — the same mature woman, this time all grown up, full of love, passion, and appreciation for herself.

SETTING

The same imaginary stage holds three podiums, each showing parts of her life.

TIME

A scene out of space and time.

ACT III

SCENE 2

SETTING: The same three podiums are placed on center stage. Each one is hidden behind a velvet curtain.

AT RISE: Again, hovering over each podium, a dazzling golden light shines; the rest of the stage remains black, like a void in the universe.

HER (VO)

This stage is my life.

All at once, I am all.

All is me.

I am one.

(Lights go off all of a sudden; the stage is obscure)

HER (VO cont.)

I am a wife; I'm a mother.

(A white light shines over the first podium to the left, the velvet curtain drops to the floor)

(The podium reveals her sitting next to her husband on the orange couch, holding hands, both of them smiling, looking behind them, where their daughter and son stand, looking back at them, joy could just burst out of this portrait)

HER (VO cont.)

I've been a mother for so long.

My hands fed my family.

My words bound it with care.

Through times of joy and despair.

(The portrait continues as the light shines over the podium to the right)

HER (VO cont.)

I'm an inspiration.

(The curtain of this podium drops to the floor)

(She's on a stage, the podium shows, sitting on an armchair in front of a huge audience. A 40-year-old woman sits in front of her; they both exchange laughs while the audience gives HER a standing ovation)

HER (VO cont.)

I'm a woman.

Shaped by pain and misery.

Trials and torments traced my path.

But I chose to forge wisdom from the past.

Transformed my lessons into refined skills.

Walking amidst beauty's vibrant flow.

Passing on my hard-earned gifts, bestow.

My words traverse realms with grace.

Carrying keys to positive parenting.

Guiding people to the core of their hearts.

I'm ever-present.

An empowering spirit prevails.

A constant force.

> (While both portraits continue, a light shines over the center podium)

HER (VO cont.)

I'm an artist.

(the podium's curtain falls to the ground, exposing HER in a musical; she's stunning, shines more than a million galaxies colliding, and is at her fullest).

HER (VO cont.)

I've always been an artist.

Destined to captivate and take control.

I'm a singer, with each note.

Worshipping every frequency from my throat.

I sing for love, for peace.

I sing for the essence of life.

Honoring joy and pain with melodious strife.

I'm an actress.

My body sways, twirls, and dances.

Amid the hallowed stage's aged allure.

I adore the scent of wood, timeless and pure.

I'm never bothered by the lights.

The more, the merrier.

For I embody my character with grace.

And rest in life's warm embrace.

(BLACKOUT)

HER (VO cont.)

This is my unyielding decree.

No curtains shall close; I'm forever free.

An open book, my essence laid bare.

In my element, I let the world stare.

For I reclaim what's mine.

Showcasing my truth and letting it shine.

On a singular stage, my spirit unfolds.

Countless roles wait in stories untold.

(BLACKOUT)

(END OF ACT III)

THE BRIDGE

In 2014, life took a dramatic turn when I received a breast cancer diagnosis, which forced me to confront a harsh reality: "To exist or to exit?"

At that point, I had already become an NLP trainer and life coach, well acquainted with the power of positive thinking and the mechanisms that cause our emotions to affect our bodies. Life had already given me the tools I needed to help me lift myself from depression to a place of recovery, rediscovery, and celebration. While I had no idea at the time that these were exactly what I needed, once the truth dawned on me, I had to apply them to myself.

Since then, dear Emiku, I have vowed to establish a profound relationship with myself to facilitate healing. I started asking myself daily, "How am I feeling today? How is my body responding?" This communication with my body became crucial for my healing journey.

Since a young age, my mother has installed precious words in my mind that have become a steady anchor and reminder to me. They were an idiom in Arabic that meant that no matter the challenges I faced, I'd always land on my feet and stand tall. This wisdom empowered me to seek solutions actively during my hard journey of self-healing, which was deeply connected to my purpose. Embracing my calling brought healing, and nothing else seemed to matter anymore.

On the shores of my homeland, when tears seemed impossible to release, surrendering allowed my voice to break free. For once, I heard the beauty of my voice, a liberating moment that echoed my soul's emancipation.

FROM SURVIVOR TO HERO

After defeating cancer heroically by reconnecting with my true self and choosing to gift myself the greatest life possible, I found in myself the passion to support other women, too. So, I became an activist in women's empowerment and launched a three-year-long campaign for breast cancer.

I named the campaign "I am not a survivor, I am a hero" because words matter.

Words influence our state of mind, Emiku. Survivors have been in a survival mindset, functioning based on survival mechanisms that marinate the body in stress. However, the hero embodies courage, strength, resilience, and a willingness to undertake extraordinary feats for the greater good. They often embark on a transformative journey, facing numerous challenges and overcoming obstacles to achieve their goals or save others. The hero represents the idealized version of a protagonist who embodies virtues and values that inspire and resonate with audiences, symbolizing the triumph of good over evil and the potential for personal growth and heroism within each individual.

THE SUPERPOWER

Along my journey of self-discovery, as my nonnegotiable self-devotion and expanding self-remembrance merged and gained momentum, I tapped into my superpower - or it tapped into me. And behold an unprecedented kind of freedom and aliveness, which I never thought possible and which I could never adequately describe, shot up in my veins and fiercely uprooted all remaining doubt, fear, shame, and guilt like a great tsunami or a massive nuclear bomb sweeping an entire empire off the face of the earth.

This emancipating power was a longstanding talent of mine. It was present in the majority of my childhood dreams and fantasies. And guess what, Emiku. When my superpower liberated me, it also became my tool for liberating others.

My superpower was my voice, and the only seer or, in this case, the only hearer who ever identified it as such was my mother. When I was still a child, she recognized how joyful and free my singing made me. Mom Alice helped me practice it and then set me off on my journey as a professional singer. I sang on stages both in Lebanon and Dubai until she passed away.

Choked with grief and pain that was insurmountable at the time, I buried this super part of me. And it took me fourteen years and yet another final round of crushing events to squeeze it out of me. When she left, I believed she had taken my voice with her. However, in reality, it was the other way around. When I accepted Life as it was and finally made peace with her death, the scales on my eyes fell off, and I realized that she had left her voice in me. As I surrendered to this truth, I could open my mouth and sing again. As I dared to retrieve my magic, my magic dared to retrieve me.

FROM THE SEED UP TO THE TRUNK

If your essence is the seed and the hidden parts of your life are the roots, then the primary expression of your essence, its original incarnation, constitutes the tree's trunk. The trunk encompasses the aspects of your existence that are perceivable to you and the world around you. They include your unique physical characteristics, your style, your body language, your actions, your facial expressions, your personality traits, your attitude, your voice, your tone, your spoken and written words, your art, your music, your superpower...

IF YOU HAD IT ALL

For the length of this magical journey, Planet Earth is fully accessible to you, Emiku. It is entirely yours. Relax in your chair as you inhale the oxygen around you and exhale your thoughts. Keep on inhaling and exhaling until your mind is quiet and clear.

It's your favorite season of the year, Emiku. The weather is just perfect. Notice how good your body feels. You are in your favorite place, wearing the clothes that most harmoniously reflect your unique essence. Notice how comfortable you feel. Right before you appear, a world-class chef could prepare the most mouth-watering, nutritious, and delicious dish for you. Go ahead, plunge in, and savor every bite. Notice how satisfied your taste buds are.

Now, feeling good and full, you look around you. All your favorite things are here in this space for you, with you, surrounding you. You smile as you feel blessed and loved. And now, all the things you ever wished to have started taking form around you. All the tools you desire to use to express your genius, talents, and skills. All the books you wanted to read, all the animals you would have loved to meet, all the pieces of art that you craved to contemplate, the best music your ears might enjoy. You sigh and expand as you feel powerful and abundant.

Take a moment and bask in the beauty and pricelessness of this moment, Emiku. Notice how lucky you feel to be here. In this place, you can be and do whatever you want.

What are you doing? Who are you being?

THE UNIVERSE INSIDE YOUR SKULL

When you were a child, Emiku, you used another super tool to make sense of yourself and the world around you and unleash your unique creativity and ability to solve problems. You used your imagination. Ironically, again, as your mind developed and you started spending more time at school and work, you likely dismissed imagination for shameful stupidity and mistook symbolic images as pointless fantasy. Your under-practiced imagination may have left you trapped in the rusty labyrinths of logic and reason, as is the gloomy fate of that good portion of humanity, which lost its balance by getting too obsessed with the realistic yet incomplete methods of the sciences.

If you could preserve and grow your childlike imagination amidst the rigidity and the objectivity, allow me to celebrate you and your brave, youthful spirit again. How heartwarming it is to see you carrying the torch of hope, possibility, and true evolution of our species. I thank you, Emiku. However, if your fire got extinguished by the choking pressure of the protocols and the formulas inundating your environment, grieve not, Emiku. When I lost all hope to regain my flame, I rose again from the ashes like a Phoenix, and I am here with you to witness your resurrection.

THE ACTOR'S MANY ROLES

In the realm of Theater, to successfully play different characters in different movies, actors usually put their raw selves aside and embody the character they're assigned, literally putting it on like putting on a costume.

They familiarize themselves well with their character's profile, and their lines become so ingrained in their minds that they recite them impeccably. They can go beyond and improvise as if their story character was truly alive through their body.

Similarly, when we choose to view Life as a Play and decide to embody our essence in all of the roles we fill, each character we play becomes a mere extension of who we are. It is not a mask that we put on, hiding our identity and truth, but rather a costume that we wear that remains faithful to our essence while reflecting the character or role that we're playing.

Same face, different clothes. Same essence, different roles.

FROM THE TRUNK UP TO THE BRANCHES

If the tree trunk is the seed's primary visible expression, your character is your essence's primary incarnation. The branches and twigs that grow out of that trunk reflect the different secondary embodiments of your essence or the roles you assumed in the past, as well as those that you currently assume and hope to assume in the future.

When the roots are deep and the tree is strong and secure, the healthy branches sprouting from the trunk grow nourishing and delicious fruits that other organisms feed upon and enjoy. In other words, when you loyally and healthily embody your essence in all the roles you play, your actions and words become your gifts of healing, service, and joy to the world around you.

YOUR MANY ROLES

Close your eyes once again, Emiku, and breathe. Breathe some more as you focus your attention on the expansion and deflation of your lungs. Breathe deeper. Relax your mind as you send your precious thoughts on a break. Now is your time to tune in with the truth within you again. Relax even further.

Now, put your hands out with your palms facing upward. Feel their thickness. Now, shift your focus to your palms. Feel their vibrating aliveness. One, two, and three... a big album lies in your hands. It was delicately handcrafted just for you. Your name is carved on its thick cover made from genuine brown leather. Feel it. Smell it. As you open it gently, you notice photos of you in different contexts doing different things. This album represents all the roles you have played so far. Flip through the photos of the Past section. Contemplate them slowly and non-judgmentally. Now, move to the photos and fill out the Present section. Notice the emotions that these photos trigger in you. Beneath every photo, there's an empty line.

Which role does it represent? Which
title would you give it?

Tip - Endings

The ending of a scene is a prerequisite for the beginning of another.
Endings are blessings.

"I am devoted to the faithful embodiment of my essence."

Chapter Four

Prep Your Stage
Do It With Love

DURING MY LIFE, I've been put on stages chosen, designed, and furnished by others... This did not serve me well.

Sometimes, we fail to embody our essence in every role we assume due to our environment. Our physical spaces might impede us... Many times throughout the years, I felt the urge to leave the places I found myself in. I wanted to run away and never look back. I found myself in places where I didn't belong, and I was searching for Home. At other times, I felt an unbeatable need to clear out my disharmonious closet and fill it up with new clothes that my character would feel good and glad to wear. But I never did out of fear of judgment and rejection.

However, when I reconnected to my essence and started embodying it in the world, I assumed responsibility for the spaces I existed in and became the designer and director of my own stages.

Drumroll...

In this Act, beloved Emiku, it is my honor to show you how to prep your stage!

"I am because of where I am."

DRAMATIS PERSONAE

ACT IV - SCENE 1

HER - a woman, all messed up, not being able to make sense of her physical environment.

SETTING

Her living room.

TIME

The scene represents every single day of her life when she lived in a place she didn't choose nor furnish herself.

ACT IV

SCENE 1

SETTING: the stage is an absurd tableau. A couch lies center stage; it's green, and its legs elongated to a comical extent, making it impossible to climb and sit on it. There's a window behind the couch; on it, a TV is defiantly hung upside down. A dining table is set to the left of the towering couch; the table is tilted precariously, making it almost impossible for a cup to find respite on its surface. Surrounding the table, a crew of three-legged chairs valiantly attempt to maintain their equilibrium. Behind the dining table, seventeen portraits are hung overlapping, with the backs of their frames jutting outward. Hovering above them, on the ceiling, garish carpets are haphazardly affixed. On the floor, metallic spirals emerge every fifty centimeters, ascending towards dark orange light bulbs. In the backdrop, stairs descend from the upper floor, their steps unnervingly yielding and pliable, while the ramp presents a treacherous path lined with thorns, where a large horizontal mirror is placed on the floor, only reaching a person's waist.

AT RISE: a disturbing symphony of non-harmonious sounds is playing; the sound is crippling as if it's playing on an old radio player. The pale light bulbs flicker.

HER

(She descends slowly from the floppy stairs and falls to her knees, arriving at the last step. She looks at her reflection in the extremely narrow mirror, SHE's a mess. SHE picks herself up and traverses the stage, SHE avoids the light bulbs spiraling from the ground and reaches the couch, SHE attempts to climb on it. SHE can't. SHE pulls a chair, puts it in front of the couch, and climbs on it, making her best effort to maintain her stability on the three-legged piece of furniture. Finally, SHE sits on the couch and discovers that there's nothing to see; the window is behind her. SHE turns around and notices the TV; SHE turns it on with the controller next to her; it's upside down, and the daylight from the window makes her vision blurry. SHE turns the TV off)

(The music stops abruptly, and the screeching sound of a ruined disc rises. The music turns on and off; it's extremely annoying)

HER

(SHE sits for moments, looking around her, SHE slides her body down the high couch and tiptoes through the light bulbs arriving at the tilted table, SHE places the controller on it, which instantly slides to the ground and collapses. SHE looks at it expressionless. SHE removes her hair from her face, and a handful of hair strands stick to her palm. SHE shakes her hands and rubs them on her thighs. SHE looks behind her where the portraits are hung. SHE approaches the wall, her back to the audience, SHE stands motionless for a few seconds, observing the backs of the frames, SHE passes her finger through them. Dust particles burst from under her finger, and SHE doesn't make any effort to clean it)

(The music stops, and voices of children calling their mothers echo all around her, accompanied by the start of what sounds like the most melancholic symphony of all times)

HER

(SHE walks backward, touches the tilted table with her hands, turns to the audience, and reaches center stage where SHE sits on the floor, and lays down on her side. SHE doesn't blink, not even once)

(BLACKOUT)

(END OF SCENE 1)

DRAMATIS PERSONAE

ACT IV - SCENE 2

She's all powered up, making her own decisions. She knows what she wants to surround herself with, and she's focused.

SETTING

The same living room.

TIME

Right after, she decided to set her own stage, which was in her best interest.

ACT IV

SCENE 2

SETTING: the stage is empty.

AT RISE: SHE is suspended above the stage by a harness around her body. In her white loose dress, she's still; a hand is up in the air, and the other surrenders to gravity.

HER

(SHE descends to the floor, SHE looks around, happy, cheerful, joyful)

(A huge orchestral symphony embarks as SHE spins in her place, smoothly, so elegantly that her being could get confused with a tornado of all that's beautiful and sweet)

HER

(SHE stops, points upstage, and makes a gesture upward with her finger. Instantly, a huge pink wall rises from the ground. From its lower left corner, a painting of a cherry tree starts to bloom amidst a flock of lovebirds scattered around)

(The music intensifies; it's a glorious serenade of her strong will, and the lights flicker harmonically with her movement throughout the scene)

HER

(SHE stands center stage, bows, and just above her head, a huge crystal chandelier descends and stops mid-air, synchronized with her bow. SHE stands back up, stretches both of her arms like wings, and snaps her fingers)

(An easel is dragged to the left of the pink wall alongside a cart full of painting material. To the right, in opposition, a round colorful rug is placed, on it, a piano takes place, and with it, the music becomes more serene)

HER

(She smirked in satisfaction, but SHE wanted more. SHE seizes the opportunity to model the stage to her liking. As the serene music stops, SHE takes a deep breath, jumps in her place, and starts to take leaps through the stage. The music accompanies her steps)

(A huge one-arm sectional is dragged center stage over which a velvet blanket falls from nowhere. To its right, seven shelves hang from the ceiling descend they're full of books, her favorite novels)

HER

(SHE jumps on the couch like a little girl; SHE rolls over and up on her feet again, takes the blanket, wraps it around herself, and throws it nonchalantly. SHE approaches the shelves and caresses the books with her left hand. SHE takes a book, smells it, and lingers in the aroma of its old pages)

(The lighting changes to a warm yellow ray showering the whole stage. It's a royal scene, one might say)

HER

(SHE puts the book on a glass table that just got dragged next to the couch, where SHE throws herself in its comfort, SHE exhales pride and fulfillment)

This is where I cry and pray.

Where I dance, lay, and paint.

Where I read and where I write.

This is where I sing, heal, and rejoice.

My pink room, where all is of me.

(BLACKOUT)

(END OF ACT IV)

HOME

In 2014, my liberation and rebirth at the shores of Lebanon marked the glorious ending of a gloomy year that my family and I had to spend in a place we called home but did not feel like home. Existing there for only one year was enough to push me far away from my essence, comfort, and passion. The symptoms of my alienation from myself were physical sickness, emotional pressure, stress, sadness, and apathy, among others.

My husband was aware of the depth and intensity of the place's impact on us. So, while I was still in Lebanon, recovering from my bruises, my husband had already closed the deal to move to our true awaited home, where I scattered myself all around the place.

I got rid of all uncomfortable furniture, broken items, nonfunctional devices, and foods that were incoherent to my desired diet and lifestyle.

THE PINK ROOM

I fulfilled all my dreams in the rooms I shared with my husband and children. But I noticed how important my privacy and time alone were. Now aware of the importance of the spaces around me, I decided to go further and build my own private sanctuary, my place of inspiration, my studio... my pink room.

The pink room is a room where I put all that describes me. I painted it myself. It was all pink, glorious. I had my recording tools in, a desk to write my songs on, comfortable couches to sit on and relax, painting material, shelves, and shelves filled with my favorite books. This room was a space for healing. This is where I cried and laughed, felt insecure and empowered, and was stuck and liberated. This was a space just for me, and no one was allowed to come in unless I let them.

THE HOUSE

Stand up, please, Emiku, and look around you.

The theater includes both public and private spaces. Emiku is called the house or the auditorium where you are sitting now. This is the fully public area of the theater, which is only accessible to the audience—you in this case—yet inaccessible to the actors during the show, which is why I'm now up here.

As you can see, the house comprises the seats from which the guests watch the performance and the other public sections, such as the box office where tickets are sold, the lobbies, the cloakroom, and the restrooms.

THE STAGE

This platform here is the only public area of the theater that is accessible to the actors while being visible yet inaccessible to the audience.

Obviously, this is where the show takes place, my dear. This space is meant to reflect the different scenes' scenery and specific physical environment. As you have noticed, each scene I performed for you so far has a unique stage set and décor conveying a specific context, a distinct mood, and an intentional message. What unspoken things have they helped you learn about me until now?

So, a good director carefully studies the script and ensures that the set adequately and intimately reflects the star's imperceivable inner states of being, such as their personality traits, lifestyle, challenges, perceptions, and states of mind. This is done through the symbolic yet well-calculated use of backgrounds, props, colors, lights, furniture, empty spaces, sound effects, and silences.

Thus, when contemplating a stage set, ask yourself:

What's the ratio of occupied spaces versus empty spaces? How are they distributed?

Which colors are dominant? Which objects are present?

How tidy and organized is the space?

How intense are the lights? What and whom do they feature?

Is the mood warm and welcoming or dry and hostile? What does it trigger in you? What do all these symbols express? What messages do they convey?

How coherent is this set with the perceivable aspects of the main character's essence?

THE STAGES OF LIFE

In your Life Theater, Emiku, the stage is any public place where you may have an audience. This means that you definitely have several stages. Some of them are controllable, and some others are not.

The uncontrollable stages are when the public might find you say a few things about you, whether you intentionally and consciously choose to be there or not. They encompass the street and building where you live, your school, your workplace, the restaurant you regularly visit... and when not too lucky, your family home and own bedroom.

On the other hand, Emiku, your controllable stages are the spaces that could expose many intricate and intimate things about you, whether you intentionally and consciously design and organize them or not. Such stages include your desk or work area, car, accessible social media profiles... and, when lucky enough, the different public rooms in your home, such as your living room and the guests' restroom.

The first thing a good director expects upon entering a new theater is that all areas will be tidied up and decluttered from the remnants of previous shows. Launching a new show from an outdated and incoherent stage set will definitely cause confusion among the actors and the audience, too. The same applies to you. So, it's not about whether the furniture is beautiful and fancy or not, but whether it survives its purpose for the scene and fills its space coherently and harmoniously with the entire set.

PUBLIC INTERVENTION

Now, please climb up these few steps, Emiku. I want you to come up and stand here with me on stage. Take a moment and contemplate the view from up here. Notice how different standing on stage feels from sitting in one of those many chairs among the audience. Sit on the floor, Emiku, right here in the middle of this stage. Close your eyes and breathe in as you feel the texture and warmth of the wooden floor beneath you. Feel its firmness and trust it as it supports your body with love.

Contemplate your various sets, your office, your home, your car... All unnecessary items, incoherent props, and irrelevant objects must be put away, clearing up the space for all the new stuff needed for the next show.

What did your environment say
about you?

Tip – Enjoy

> Even if getting rid of some objects might be painful, insist on keeping your beautiful smile on. Decluttering your environment is a precious expression of growth and abundance.

THE GAPS

Sometimes, when observing the stage sets, we find gaps. They are usually proof of incoherence between our authentic essence and the character or role that we are assuming. They are alarms signaling that we're out of character and are now executing an empty audience-centered performance rather than expressing and embodying our true essence through our vessel called our character. These gaps usually are gracious symptoms indicating that one or more lessons are asking to be learned.

When you notice them, Emiku, look closely and ask yourself: What am I trying to prove and to whom? What fears or insecurities are driving me? Which parts of my show are mere performances aiming to entertain or please my audience?

THE BACKSTAGE

The backstage area, also called the offstage, is the theater's fully private space. It is only accessible to the actor, the director, the scriptwriter, and the backstage crew. The audience is inaccessible and totally out of sight.

The backstage is situated right behind the walls of the stage and consists of several parts. The dressing room is where we find the shower, the locker, the vanity table, the costumes, the mirror, and such. The green room is the lounge area where the actors rest, meditate, refuel, and rehearse their lines. Other props, furniture, and equipment are kept in the storage area.

In our Life Theater, beloved Emiku, these private spaces are where we take breaks from the outside noise to reconnect with ourselves and grow. In there, we expand our knowledge, practice our skills, optimize our talents, and tune our instruments.

We seek these places to find the privacy and resources needed to diligently sculpt, rehearse, and polish our character and recharge the energy and inspiration needed to write, review, and edit our script perseveringly.

Our offstage areas could be our room, bathtub, reading chair, sacred sanctuary, car, secret spot in the park, or maybe our favorite activities. Our supporting material sometimes takes the form of a good book, an inspirational sticky note, a challenging course, an anchoring reminder, a little nothing of great sentimental value, a line in a commercial song, a random post on social media, a quote hung on the bathroom wall of an old restaurant, or the resounding words of a late parent.

THE BACKSTAGE, TOO, PLAYS A ROLE

Since the seed is your essence and the roots are your life experiences, the tree's climate and soil represent the physical environments where you form your experiences. An optimal physical environment equips the tree to reach its greatest genetic potential, grow in the healthiest manner possible, and ultimately yield the best fruits it could ever bear. Similarly, when you experience life in optimal physical environments, Emiku, your essence gets to manifest itself in the healthiest and most authentic ways possible.

When you perform your life story on the greatest stages, it becomes possible for you to have your greatest life show ever. And when you rest, practice, and grow in the best backstages, you gift yourself the chance to reach your character's greatest potential. Now, since such optimal abiotic variables rarely exist by themselves, it is very helpful for you to pay attention to your current and future physical environments, even if the tree was originally planted in poor conditions.

To improve a fruit tree's physical environment, it might be necessary to start by cleaning its soil and getting rid of all the waste that might be found there. This would also include removing dead roots, big rocks, and other obstacles that might hinder it from growing well. In some cases, the plant might need to be transferred to another soil or a bigger pot.

Now, in the world of Theater, a professional director wouldn't only expect the public areas of the theater to be clean and clear but also the private spaces. Thus, decluttering the stage alone is not enough, for launching a new show from a chaotic backstage swamped with irrelevant props and old tools will waste precious time and energy among both the actors and the crew members. And again, the same applies to you, dear Emiku.

PRIVATE INTERVENTION

Walk with me to the offstage areas, Emiku, and look around. This is your life's backstage.

Check the props. What's missing? Does it feel like you need many things that are missing? Bring them in and mark them out the way you like. Highlight them on your stage. After doing so, take a step back and check things up. Is it exactly the way you want them to be? How do I want my stage to be furnished and decorated? What colors will be on my walls, and what shades will be on my face?

Close your eyes and notice: What's dusty? Clean it up. What's rusty? Release it. And I mean, actually, throw stuff away. Go to your room, open your closet, and get rid of what doesn't suit you anymore. Observe your shelves. What needs to be cleaned? What needs to be released with love and forgiveness?

Tip – Apply

The greatest benefit from all mental exercises is extracted when manifested in real-life applications.

THE FOURTH WALL

In the theater, an invisible barrier, the Fourth Wall, stands between the house and the stage. Its purpose is to ensure the smooth and uninterrupted flow of the play by separating the people serving the story from those unrelated to it. The actor may intentionally break the Fourth Wall when it is part of the story. However, it sometimes improperly collapses when order is insufficiently established or when the distracted actor breaks out of character.

In your life theater, Emiku, this means that sometimes it may be necessary and beneficial to avoid acting and interacting with the audience present in your life. The audience is not actors; the only suitable interaction with them is greeting them and bowing to them when your show is over.

SLIPPING OUT OF DALIDA

In 2016, I was asked to perform Dalida on stage at The Music Hall. An entire orchestra was spread out behind me, and thousands of people were filling up the house. I was wearing a wig of long blond curved hair and a glittery dress, and put on makeup that made me resemble her so closely to impersonate her as best as possible.

Before the curtains opened, I was Dalida. But when they opened, and the audience saw me, they started shouting my name: "Nadine! Nadine! Nadine!" And there, under the spotlights, Nadine was summoned back, and the Fourth Wall was breached as I interacted with them. For a few seconds, Dalida was gone.

Of course, the orchestra did not stop playing. However, I did and got totally disconnected from what was happening. I forgot where I was and what I was meant to do. It was scary and hard to reconnect to Dalida and reembody her.

During your transformational journey of building your character, people from your past will remind you of who you were. Remember to remain present, Emiku. Remain diligently and fully in character. Remain focused and avoid falling back into that past version of yourself. Otherwise, as life continues playing its notes, you'll find yourself out of beat and out of tune.

The Fourth Wall in your life, Emiku, represents your boundaries. It is this bubble that you create around you that filters all that happens outside of you.

Your Boundaries

At certain points in our lives, we may find ourselves totally dissatisfied with one of our stages, or more, and may wish to leave without ever looking back. This usually happens if our stage stops being inaccessible to our public and people randomly come up on our stage and interfere with our setting... or when we've tried to adapt for too long to an uncontrollable environment that is toxic to us... or when we've evolved big and quick, and our physical entourage becomes totally out of sync with the new story and character.

In such cases, as yourself:

- Is the audience of this stage appropriate for my show?

- Does it respect my Fourth Wall?

- How can I fortify my own boundaries?

- Do I feel safe and secure in these stages?

- Is leaving necessary?

If the answer is yes and you are able to leave, think of practical steps to move forward with your decision.

However, if leaving is either unnecessary or impossible for the time being, ensure your mental and physical health and check for practical steps to help you keep going on:

- How could I take a break from this place?

- What small tweaks can I do around me?

- Could adding a new item or removing an old one be enough for now?

- Am I able to redecorate or refurnish?

- Am I able to do a total makeover?

"I am devoted to the continuous enhancement of my stage."

Chapter Five

Write Your Script

Reveal Yourself

THE DEEPER I RECONNECTED to my essence, the more my sovereignty was restored.

Once the mediocre characters I had previously consented to play drowned in the Mediterranean Sea, I was finally free to become the star of my life. I threw to the wind the ripped pieces of all the scripts I had clung to for decades for fear of ending up abandoned in the shadows of some deserted backstage. My hands were finally empty, and my heart was brave enough to hold the pen and start writing my script.

As I gradually remembered who I was and got fine-tuned to the harmony of my song, I learned how to discern the dissonant notes that crept into my symphony. I took on the challenge of defining and refining my character. Being my own greatest asset and the only unfailing one, I zealously crowned myself the star of my show. Then, I decided how my story would unfold by seriously assuming my role as the Genie in My Lantern, the composer of my melody, and the writer of my play.

Drumroll...

In this Act, sweet Emiku, it is my utmost pleasure and honor to present the steps to writing your own script!

"As long as my hourglass still contains a grain of sand,

the orchestra playing my song shall follow my command.

As long as the wind spins the blades of my mill,

My right hand shall surely hold the feather quill."

DRAMATIS PERSONAE

ACT V - SCENE 1

HER — a distorted young woman who can't make her own decisions; other people's opinions lead her.

OLD MAN - a representative of judgments that a person can only be one thing and not express their true desires.

OLD WOMAN - a representative of an ancient mentality that kids must be raised in a way that breaks their dreams and passions.

GENTLEMAN - a representative of stubborn logic, neglecting the importance of love in what a person does.

GROUP OF GIRLS - a representative of envy, selfishness, and taking advantage of others.

MAN - a representative of the idea that only a person's properties matter.

LADY - a representative of the idea that only physical appearances matter.

SETTING

An imaginary stage in her mind.

TIME

Every single time throughout her life, other people have influenced her self-expression.

ACT V

SCENE 1

SETTING: the stage is enveloped in a shroud of darkness. A huge ancient mirror stands center stage. Gigantic fingerprints are all over it, distorting the image it reflects to the extent that one could confuse their reflection with another person. Surrounding the central mirror, four smaller mirrors cast an eerie symmetrical pattern. Like fog on an autumn night, these mirrors form a chilling square, each reflecting distorted fragments of a soul lost to time, heavy with melancholy.

AT RISE: She stands in front of the center mirror, her back to the mirror. She faces the audience. Dressed in tattered garments, she is disheveled. Her gaze is fixated upon the emptiness looming before her, a void echoing helplessness and shattered hopes.

HER

(Parts her lips to talk)

(A clash of cymbals resonates, and the first mirror to her left illuminates, within its depth emerges the grotesque visages of an aged MAN and WOMAN. SHE remains resolute)

OLD MAN

Little girl, hold your tongue; you've assumed the mantle of a housewife, which demands sacrifice and selflessness. Abandon your frivolous pursuits, for they are nothing but foolish dreams. There's no room for your own desires. Keep your attention within the four walls of your home. The time for indulgence has expired.

OLD WOMAN

(Replies as soon as he finishes)

Think of your kids. It is unjust to deny them the disciplined upbringing they deserve. What stupidity are you entangled in? We hold well-established customs and a deeply ingrained culture. This isn't how we raise our offspring. First, be more firm with them, for their success reflects your own. Stop giving them the freedom of being, for they are your legacy and heritage. Finally, control them, for they don't know what's best for them.

(Again, cymbals clang loudly, and the first mirror to her right blazes with light. Within its frame emerges a gentleman's face)

GENTLEMAN

Let's not lose sight of the real problem, shall we? Or perhaps everyone is as oblivious as she is? I'll enlighten you, ma'am. Abandon the futile notion of artistic endeavors; it serves no purpose. Rely on reason, for the heart will only lead you astray. Go ahead and get yourself a regular job. You've always excelled at crunching numbers and organizing paperwork. You enjoyed it. You're skilled at it. Come on, it's obvious.

(As he concludes, cymbals ring again through the air. The second mirror to her left bursts into illumination. A group of young women pops up. Their appearance mirrors the flawless perfection showcased in glossy magazines)

GIRLS

(Speak in unison)

Oh my goodness, can we all stop being so hard on her? Hey, don't you worry! We've got your back! You're a symbol of popularity, beauty, talent, and wealth. Also, you know everyone worth knowing. These "loyal" friends you hang out with don't seem to add glitter to your life. Clear your schedule tomorrow; we're having lunch to spill the tea!

(As they echo empty giggles, a jarring clash of cymbals reverberates. In defiant opposition, the second mirror to her right blazes to light. Two faces materialize, revealing the weary presence of a couple dressed to the nines, a MAN and a LADY)

MAN

(Addressing the group of girls)

Are you really considering spending time with her? Have you seen her house? What a disaster. And don't get me started on that unpleasant ambiance. And the furniture is just a mess. Who cares if it's comfortable and personalized, darling? It's all about appearances. You better get someone to redecorate for you, or else what will people think?

LADY

And look at her hair. Who do you think you are, parading around in that abomination? I swear, if I were caught wearing something like that, I'd pass out. Take my advice, sweetheart; it's time to revamp your looks. Look at me, take a lesson, I'll book a slot for you at my salon, chop chop.

(Amidst the faint hum of whispered talks resonating from the mirrors, their voices blending into a suspenseful chorus. In perfect synchronization, the identical monologues reverberate endlessly. Suddenly, a hairline fracture starts to propagate across the reflective surface of the central mirror)

(With orchestral precision, thin, translucent strings emerge from each mirror, tying her wrists and ankles. The strings pull in an opposing direction, stretching her body. SHE begins to ascend. Suspended mid-air, her limbs tugged by invisible hands, SHE's now a marionette caught in a tangled web of fate imposed upon her)

(Out of nowhere, a resounding crescendo fills the place, as the central mirror behind her shatters into a thousand shards, showering the stage, and casting a surreal kaleidoscope of confusion. HER body goes limp, consciousness slipping away as she drifts into the realm of unconsciousness, like a fragile dream)

(BLACKOUT)

(END OF SCENE 1)

DRAMATIS PERSONAE

ACT V - SCENE 2

HER - an empowered woman who decided to take the wheel of her life, not caring about other people's nagging and criticism.

SETTING

The same imaginary stage in her mind.

TIME

Right after, she decided to do what pleased her.

ACT V

SCENE 2

SETTING: the stage is dark once more. The central mirror's ruins remain on the floor. The four other mirrors surround it; they flicker a white flashing light. The faces they once exposed are motionless.

AT RISE: SHE's still suspended mid-air. Her hands and legs stretch like a sea star; SHE's unconscious.

HER

(A bright glorious white light blooms just behind her. Accompanied by a symphony playing "L'hymne à l'amour", SHE awakens mid-air. With an abrupt motion of determination, SHE pulls the threads with all the power SHE could assemble, causing the four mirrors surrounding her to crash all at once, demolishing the faces they once bared)

(Sequentially, a huge bright mirror, identical to the last one descends behind HER. Unlike its worn-out predecessor, this piece is embraced by a golden frame, diamonds flicker here and there on each side)

(As the mirror settles on the ground, the music seizes. SHE descends to the floor. It's all quiet)

(Her eyes are of fire. Her spirit soars, it's just obvious. With a head held high, SHE cracks a smile of a conqueror. SHE is her own master in her puppet show. In the palm of her hand lies a quill, and in the other sleeps an empty leaf)

HER

(SHE turns around and takes a look. The looking glass shines and is just so clear that SHE can see her deepest wells, her sharpest edges, the things that go unnoticed, and all that SHE aspires to be. SHE's no longer a wind-up doll. SHE is the carpenter, the mechanic, the tailor, and the painter. SHE's in control. It feels good)

(BLACKOUT)

(END OF ACT V)

ON THE SANDY SHORE

Right after my surgery and my journey of cancer treatments, I decided that it was time for me to heal. So, I took on the quest to do all that it takes to break through. Usually, breakthroughs happen through crying, shouting, and other forms of expression of all the suppressed emotions. So, I booked a hotel room at a beach resort to be alone and have a date with God to understand my purpose on earth. "Why am I here?" I asked, "And why am I going through these challenges?"

I started recreating painful scenarios in my mind to stimulate myself to cry and bring all my anger out. Yet, this did not work.

It was cold that night, and the wind was very strong. Still, my suffocation was so intense that I put on my coat, left the room, and walked toward the sea, my life-long refuge.

I stood at the shore, yet was so exhausted that I could no longer ask myself any questions, Emiku... I just surrendered. I surrendered to the sound of the crashing waves, the wind blowing all around me, and the coldness of the air. I let go, and time ceased to exist. Suddenly, I was in a trance.

I woke up from it to my voice, loud and fierce, singing l'Hymne A l'Amour by Edith Piaf as tears streamed down my face. I finally cried, yet the catalyst of my catharsis was my voice.

With no exceptions, Emiku, we all have our own healing tool within us. To find them, all we have to do is take a deep breath and surrender. To enter the state of flow that artists, writers, and creative people tap into to release and sublimate their emotions, revealing their innermost essence.

My essence is creativity. It is about using my voice and writing. This is why, when I was emancipated, I decided to express my emotions artistically for the first time. I decided I wasn't going to hide or shy away anymore. So, I planned to write this book and inspirational songs that always lived within me, inspired by my life experiences and the stories I heard around me. With each song, I released a part of me waiting to be set free.

When I reconnected with my talent and my voice, I used it to sublimate my emotions and combine my life lessons into a work of art that healed me and inspired others.

PUPPET OR MASTER?

For most days, dear Emiku, I was mainly a puppet pulled by different invisible threads to me...

As I woke up on the shores of Lebanon, I felt suffocated by the strings I'd been attached to. This acted like a huge shift in my life, and we, as human beings, are often afraid of change. Despite that, I cut them off. This is when I felt free for the first time. I embraced my past, embodied my essence, chose my roles selectively, and fixed my body accordingly.

A puppet comes into existence with no backstory or essence of its own. The puppet master gives these to the puppet. If several masters use the puppet, it ends up having several backstories and different essences coherent with each master's story.

Now, since the doll might play different unrelated and incoherent roles written and chosen by the masters, it represents the puppet masters' desires, wearing their chosen clothes.

A puppet has a body and a physical form, yet it also has no control over it. Eventually, the masters seem to decide what to wear and how to appear on behalf of the puppet.

My vision suddenly got clearer on that sandy shore, and I could see them all. Fueled by my loyalty and unbendable resilience, I broke them all.

Aware, I cut the strings, which gave my previous masters power over me. I was no longer a passive object used by others at their will. I woke up, stood up, and took into my hands the proactive responsibility of choosing who I am and deciding which roles I would play and the following chapters of my life. Having become the scriptwriter of my own life story, I first wrote my character's profile.

A CHARACTER'S PROFILE

In the realm of Theater, the information that census surveys provide are found in what we call "a character profile". In a good character profile, the proficient playwright elaborates all they know about the character, giving the actor enough material to answer the question "Who am I?" spontaneously and exhaustively. The more detailed and comprehensive the description is, the greater the odds are to behold an exquisite script, a flawless story, and an outstanding performance – the genuine incarnation of the character.

Thus, a good character profile not only includes the categories found in census surveys, such as the character's origins, physical appearance, backstory, and major achievements but goes beyond them to encompass all the things that fundamentally make up the character's essence.

In real life, Emiku, we're meant to embody our own essence and not create it, embracing all the facets of reality. Thus, writing a Character's Profile in real life is about describing the past and not reinventing it. It's about discovering our unique essence, not borrowing bits and pieces from others around us and pretending to be what we're not.

SCRIPTS, SCRIPTS, SCRIPTS...

When a tree grows up in a crowded space, the things in its environment play a huge role in deciding how it grows and in which direction. So, the growth of a tree planted right next to a fence or a wall gets dictated by the fence: it diverts when it faces the obstacle as if the obstruction is telling it "not from here" or grows between the bars of the fence. Or this diversion might be caused by the presence of other plants and animals.

Similarly, when you allow the people in your life to edit your life play's script and modify your sets, my dear, you are granting them access to your director's chair, and thus giving them the right to decide on your behalf what your life show will be about and how it will look like.

In other words, when you lend your quill to any other person, you would give up on your main responsibility as your own life's scriptwriter: writing your own script. And when you do that, you would be sacrificing all sovereignty and control over your life, losing your other rights as your own life director and, ultimately, your role as the main character in your story. You end up performing others' scripts. However, I am certain that this is not what we want, for we each yearn to be the masters of our own lives.

THE REFINEMENT

Sit back, Emiku, and breathe deeply again for a few seconds. Then, ask yourself:

- If I were the master of my own life, who would I be?

- What would it look like if I could rewrite my story from a Play perspective? What lessons does my backstory teach me?

- How would I build my character? How would I fill out my character's profile?

- What are the roles that I would love to keep on playing? How would I enhance them?

Tip - Dare

The idea that possibilities exist beyond the familiar can be pretty scary. Dare to dive into the waters, for the way will light up for you as you go.

My Character's Profile

My Backstory:

My Essence:

My Body:

My Roles:

My Next Life-Chapter

Lay your back against your seat now, Emiku, and take a deep breath as you ready yourself for a new adventure.

The door to an ultra-futuristic capsule opens before you. Awestruck, you contemplate its sleek lines and neon lights. As you step onto it, and before you even process it, you find yourself teleported a few pages forward in your life script, to a time in the near future, to your next life chapter.

What does your next life chapter look like?

Take a deep breath in, sweet one. Open your eyes and start jotting down all the thoughts and images that cross your mind, led by the flow of your intuition. This time, you won't set any alarms; you are invited to keep writing until you are totally out of words.

Tip - Unleash

To imagine and to dream is to be human. Open your mind, unleash your creativity, and allow your nature to take over.

Location:

Time:

Role:

State of Mind:

Purpose:

> *"I am devoted to the endless re-fining of my script."*

Chapter Six

Your Support Crew

Your Backbones

IN THIS WORLD, WE cannot do it all alone. We need each other just as the actors need their support crew.

Our species survived and evolved by being social and interdependent. Unless we choose to go off the grid and live with basic wildlife in the forest, it is almost impossible for us to survive solo in the world today. Thus, no matter how much we try to convince ourselves that we can do it alone, our backbone people are necessary in our lives, and chances are, they've always been there.

These people are the ones who love us unconditionally and are there for us when we need to be heard, seen and understood. They are the ones who recognize our different life seasons and hold space for us when we are transitioning from one state of mind to the other, one chapter to the other, one version to the other. They are the ones who do so without trying to influence us with their own opinions and ideas but rather serve as catalysts to bring out the best in us.

Drumroll...

In this Act, sweet Emiku, it is my utmost pleasure and honor to present your beautiful support crew!

"Can you imagine a body without bones?"

DRAMATIS PERSONAE

ACT VI - SCENE 1

HER - a young lady who believed in her calling, comes face to face with the lack of wisdom in her decisions.

NEEDY – represents envious people who are willing to do whatever they can to possess what others have.

GREEDY represents greedy, ungrateful people who take advantage of other people's skills and connections.

SETTING

On a path to a destination of growth and fulfillment.

TIME

This scene combines two separate events of her life, both of which were very similar, taking place in a short period, not too long ago from the present day.

ACT VI

SCENE 1

SETTING: The forgotten ruins of an ancient fortress, moss-covered stones, and tangled vines create a peculiar atmosphere as the sunlight struggles to penetrate the ceiling above. We're amidst decaying remnants of an old place.

AT RISE: SHE stands center stage, in the middle of nowhere, holding a huge suitcase so full she could barely lift it.

HER

(Exhausted by the heat)

This is agonizing. I can't go on any longer, but I have to get this suitcase delivered; if I didn't, I would never be able to fulfill the trade I got myself into.

(Hearing her from a distance, two young people approach her. NEEDY and GREEDY dressed in black)

GREEDY

Let me help you out with this.

HER

(Stutters as she starts to feel unsafe)

NEEDY

(Reassuring)

Don't worry; he's strong enough. We're heading North; if our paths coincide, we'd be more than delighted to walk together and give you a hand.

HER

(Looks at them for a moment; they seem nice, and she can use a helping hand. She hands him the suitcase)

I'm going north too, so let's walk together then.

(The three of them walk to the left of the stage)

(Lights are off, the scenery changes, and vast sand dunes carpet the stage. The scorching sun beats down mercilessly, casting a harsh light over the barren landscape)

(They reappear from the right side of the stage)

NEEDY

So, why are you so packed heavily? What's your journey about?

HER

This is my ultimate project; I've been working my whole life to fulfill it; it's my calling. To achieve this, I have to do an exchange. I give what's in that suitcase, and I get in return what I've been longing for

GREEDY

And would you be able to share what's in it for you?

HER

(She takes a moment)

Sure, I'm doing all of this for the good of a huge community of people, people who are willing to walk the path of discovery and love.

NEEDY

That's very inspiring; I've always wanted to help people like you do.

GREEDY

Indeed, what I admire is the amount of resources one must own to be able to execute such a project. You're impressive

NEEDY

Let us accompany you; we'd love to help you more. Your calling is astonishing.

GREEDY

I'd say it's mind-blowing; what you just said expresses everything I wanted to do my whole life.

HER

(A hopeful look takes over her face)

Definitely, you're more than welcome, partners. But let's rest; I'm exhausted.

NEEDY

I could die for a nap right now.

GREEDY

Let's nap, then.

(He puts the suitcase down, and the three of them lie on the ground, SHE falls asleep instantly)

(Seconds pass, and GREEDY sits straight and stares at the suitcase. He opens it, he's stupefied, he wakes NEEDY and points to the suitcase, she closes her mouth with both her hands, she can't believe what she sees)

NEEDY

(Looks at him cunningly)

Are we on the same page here?

GREEDY

This is a treasure; this woman is a real-life treasure. Do you know what would this make of us?

NEEDY

I'd do anything to have an aura like her, and it's all in this suitcase, scattered under the palm of my hands.

GREEDY

Look at all those names, presidents, celebrities, and powerful people. Is this a joke?

NEEDY

Clearly not; this looks like a huge deal she was about to close. I won't miss this opportunity, Stafaum.

GREEDY

I've been working so hard to have contacts like these. But wait, I'm afraid that's not right.

NEEDY

We've been hungry for days, endured this long journey to arrive at your cousin's house, and are not even sure he'll help us. Let's take it all; she looks powerful enough to compensate.

GREEDY

She is tough, come on then

(They empty the suitcase in their bags quickly and flee quietly, leaving HER alone with her empty suitcase)

HER

(Wakes up, looks around, no one's there)

NEEDY? GREEDY? Guys?

HER (cont.)

(She notices her suitcase, wide open, empty as her stomach)

What the... oh no. I can't believe that this is happening to me.

(She finds a single piece of paper from the suitcase, and she reads it impatiently)

HER

We're sorry, we had to take the stuff. We need them more than you do. You're strong, and you can replenish whenever you feel like it. Goodbye.

(She throws the letter away; she closes her eyes)

Why do such circumstances persistently haunt me? I always dare to believe that virtuous people come to provide solace, only to be cruelly deceived after they discover my potential. And they betray me, robbing me to fill in what they lack. If only those two knew how many people would've been helped if I had delivered this suitcase, they would've acted differently. Apparently, our Norths are not aligned.

(BLACKOUT)

(END OF SCENE 1)

DRAMATIS PERSONAE

ACT VI - SCENE 2

HER - a mature woman, clear-minded and passionate about her calling, finally understands who she wants to have in her life.

MAN - a person she met in real life who played a role in helping her tell her stories.

WOMAN - a person she met in real life who helped her express herself.

SETTING

In a peaceful spot in nature.

TIME

This scene literally takes place in the present day.

ACT VI

SCENE 2

SETTING: a land painted in green, vibrant shades abound. In the distance, there's a glass house. It's very vast, captivating the gaze. Under the bright sun, a gentle breeze caresses serenely the tall blades of grass that scatter the scene.

AT RISE: SHE appears from the right side of the stage, holding her suitcase over her head. A worn-out MAN and WOMAN sit on the floor just a few steps from her. Their exhaustion mirrors her own. Their backpacks serve as pillows for them to sit on.

HER

I've come from a faraway land; can you please lead me to the head-quarters in this place?

MAN

(Looks up at her)

Hello, of course, it's right ahead.

(He points to the glass house)

WOMAN

Young woman, you're exhausted; what's the matter?

HER

My journey was rough; I faced many obstacles along the way

MAN

Then let us help you out; I'll hold your suitcase for you.

HER

(Recalling what happened before)

No! I can hold it by myself.

WOMAN

Sounds like you've endured rough circumstances

HER

I'm fine; lead the way, please.

MAN

(Looks at the WOMAN and smiles)

We've been resting before arriving at the same place you're going to. We've been pressing on for many years but grew old and weary, and our inspiration ran dry. We thought maybe we were not meant to arrive.

WOMAN

We worked our whole life to create these little booklets. Check them out.

(She takes a small handcrafted booklet and gives it to her)

MAN

They're small gems meant to be useful for lost people in their journey for their self-retrieval.

HER

(Surprised)

That's impressive.

WOMAN

Thank you. It has always been an uttermost pleasure and shared aspiration to perform such a meaningful gesture for the betterment of humanity.

HER

Thank you for that.

MAN

Let me help you out with your suitcase.

(SHE gives it to him, and he notices how light it is)

MAN (cont.)

This suitcase is empty, why are you carrying it then?

HER

I was betrayed and robbed by two individuals whom I considered my friends, as they took away what was rightfully mine.

WOMAN

Poor thing, here, have some water.

(Handing her a bottle)

HER

(She takes the bottle and sips some water)

MAN

Are you hungry?

(As he reaches into his bag and pulls out an apple)

MAN (cont.)

Here you go; you need some energy.

HER

I do, thank you, that's very kind.

WOMAN

You remind me of someone I knew long ago who possessed the same unwavering determination and commitment. In recognition of that, I extend to you the offer of one of our booklets.

(She hands her one)

MAN

I think I know of whom she speaks; I have long admired tenacious women, those who refuse to surrender even on the arduous road, even when their suitcases are emptied. Please accept this as a symbol of my admiration.

(He hands her a file—a very thick file—from his bag)

MAN (cont.)

Within this binder lie precious jewels of hope, unwavering belief, and steadfast support; it serves as a guiding companion, ensuring you never walk alone in your journey.

HER

(Looks at them, a tear about to fall from her eye)

WOMAN

No, no, don't you cry; look around. It's a wonderful day. Rejoice in the sunrays and bask in this sweet breeze.

MAN

Do you know? It is truly an honor to have crossed paths with you. Your presence has illuminated our day, reminding us to persevere and forge ahead despite our challenges.

HER

Is that so?

WOMAN

(Laughing)

Yes, you're not the only one who received gifts today, we have also been bestowed with a precious gift, seeing a woman as beautiful and young as you, walking alone on this road, definitely rekindled our passion. Our energies are replenished, and it's all thanks to you.

MAN

(Looks at the WOMAN with a sweet smile)

And we might as well resume our steps.

HER

(Head held high, with a composed tone)

It is my honor and pleasure... actually, this is what I'm here for. What are your names, if I may ask?

(The conversation fades away as the lights go off)

(BLACKOUT)

(END OF ACT VI)

BONELESS

Looking at my life from a bird-eye view, I can clearly notice that I moved, traveled, and changed houses and countries many times. This unstable lifestyle led me to lose many important people due to the distance between us. Then, at some point, I found myself in a new environment in which I was a total stranger.

I remember the countless times I felt homesick and lonely. I was constantly under the microscope, and I had only a few people left in my life who knew who I was and were willing to give me the support I needed. Does this resonate with you, Emiku?

I felt as if my backstage wasn't backing up my stage anymore. My crew wasn't as efficient as I desired, especially since I had no script; anyone was coming in and filling the void. The support crew that was supposed to organize my props and help me tidy my space brought props from other backstages they worked in. Despite having the best intentions at heart, being genuine, and trying to be helpful, they were counterproductive and unintentionally messing around my backstage. The props were incoherent with the scenes that I was about to play. Hence, the consequences that I had to bear were devastating.

OUTDATED CREW

Just as we depend on other people to feed our bodies, so do we depend on our support crew to feed our minds and souls. Thus, just as bakers nourish us with their bread and clients support us with their money, our backstage crew supports us even when we aren't aware of it. Our failure to notice their presence usually results from us looking at our lives through narrow close-up shots that overlook the remainder of the vast scene.

That's why it's important to keep an eye out for the people we're allowing to meddle in the backstage of our lives, even when their intentions are the purest you could ever find. They might offer or impose their support based on their perceptions of what is best for us or where they want us to be. This also applies to friends who lead lifestyles that no longer reflect our values, teachers who preach perspectives that we've outgrown, and family members who don't seem to appreciate and uphold our authentic essence truly, even if unconsciously and unintentionally.

SOME TREES DON'T GROW TOGETHER

Companion planting is planting two or more mutually beneficial plants near each other. Interestingly, companion plants can be fruits, vegetables, shrubs, flowers, herbs, and more that provide shade, nutrients, or protection from pests and diseases to neighboring plants and trees. If you have a plant or tree with specific companion needs, you can grow another nearby to ensure both plants reach their full potential.

Similarly, some backstage people don't make good companions, Emiku. And this has nothing to do with who they are and what their essence is about. This merely reflects that they and you aren't compatible puzzle pieces. So when they do get to play the role of a backstage support crew, instead of focusing on supporting you and your play, they end up snuggling in their own ideas and lines, robbing you of your own nutrients, space, and unique expression.

Thus, just as a farmer would avoid planting some trees in each other's vicinity, it would be wise of you to be selective of the people you choose to make your backbone, the ones you give access to your own backstage and most intimate spaces.

Being your own life director, remember to draw the rights, privileges, and boundaries necessary to strengthen any relationship and be of mutual service. Be selective when sharing your secrets, seeking advice, reviewing your lines, and deciding what to do next. Even the closest people to you and those you bet genuinely love you should respect your boundaries and serve your vision; otherwise, it is not true love.

UNSUPPORTIVE CREW

Sit back and relax in your chair, Emiku. Close your eyes and send a mental message inviting your current support crew members for an intimate gathering. Breathe in as their faces show up one by one. They might take different forms and sizes, appearing cartoonish and faded or seeming vibrant and real. Take note of their sequence, facial expressions, and attitude. Remember their mindsets, attitudes, and how they show up for you. Remember the things they say and do when they attempt to support you.

Who has been supporting you?
Who has not?

Tip - Blessed Triggers

Who triggers you more teaches you more...about who you are

not.

ADIEU

Beloved Emiku, go up to the control room, where all the light buttons, levers, and switches are located. Turn off all the lights and contemplate the quiet darkness. Breathe in the emptiness, and breathe out all the emotions you may have felt while doing the previous exercise.

Now, turn on the center stage light, Emiku. A glorious white light shines down on a royal white chair carefully placed in the middle of the stage - the Adieu Chair.

Hold the list of the crew members you found incompatible with your new life chapter. See them go up one by one onto the stage and sit in this royal Adieu seat.

1. **Feel & Explain:** Take a moment to feel all the emotions that the person sitting in the Adieu chair in center stage might stir in you. Bravely and objectively face the truth of their presence in your life and release any clogged emotions you might still have toward them. Every individual is indeed a beautifully unique character playing a detrimental role in this huge Play of Life, yet not all scripts and roles go together. Thus, explain to this person the reasons for this adieu, at least for now.

2. **Learn & Anchor:** Think of every lesson you may have learned thanks to them. Each lesson is a priceless gem, a precious diamond, and finding it makes digging hard in the deep and dark mine totally worth it. These are your treasures. Life's small blessings make you stronger, wiser, mature, and more yourself. Give each lesson a name or a title, feel its value, bask yourself in the emotions that it makes you feel, and anchor this feeling, record it, own it, and use it to fuel your essence, superpowers, and story.

3. **Thank & Release:** Feeling empowered and resourceful, express your genuine appreciation to the person sitting in the Adieu chair. Share with them the lesson or lessons that they helped you learn. Anchored in your learnings, smile at them as you contemplate the smooth white light coming from above them, showering them with love and gratitude. Clap for them wholeheartedly for performing their role so beautifully. The lesson is learned! Send them your best intentions and wishes, then turn off the light above them, releasing them and sending them home.

MY BACKBONE

Progressing through each event, I unraveled and unleashed the "me" buried inside. Knowing what I had to give and the gems waiting to emerge from the world, I started to appreciate the constructive, propelling input from what and who was around me.

I began to seek out new mentors, coaches, and teachers. I emptied entire shelves in my house and filled them with new kinds of books. My pink room is always jamming with blissful music, and I focus on feeding my brain with interesting, nourishing bits of information.

This personal-internal shift started to reflect itself in my choice of people to come and help me backstage.

A good support crew is faithful to the scriptwriter, director, and main actor. They serve the story wholeheartedly while keeping their own desires and imagined outcomes out of the game.

Among my beloved support crew: Serge, my husband, my best friend, and my earth angel, who proved to be my backbone year after year, challenge after challenge, and project after project. My mentor followed me during that training all the way down into the rabbit hole when all I wanted to do was escape the pain. My late mother continues to be a dear source of inspiration and support. My consultants and team believe in me and go out of their way to encourage, cheer, and support me in achieving my dreams. Despite not being a person, my belief system remains the firm foundation and safety net that always catches me when I doubt myself and refills me when I desire to give up.

THE PERFECT TEAM

In every theater's backstage, we find everything necessary for a successful show: Emiku: the backstage crew who helps run the show and ensures all goes well. These amazing people help us use our props and store them in place, they aid us in putting on our costumes and makeup, and sometimes even help us rehearse our script. And when anything goes wrong, since hazards do happen, these experts are the ones we rely on to replace our broken props, sew our torn costumes, and fix our smudged makeup.

In the backstage of our Life Theater, these beautiful people are our backbone, our support system. They are the ones who hold our vision, sharpen us, tweak us, and propel us forward. They are the people we call when we find ourselves in a crisis or emergency, and the ones who have our backs when making it through another day seem too burdensome.

Our backstage crew is our caring tribe with whom we safely share our feelings and confidently discuss our thoughts. They are our healers, our refuge, who gladly lend us an ear and humbly offer us a shoulder to cry on. They are our wise mentors, empowering coaches, and unique friends... and when we're lucky, they may be our parents, siblings, partners, and children.

And sometimes, Emiku, these people pop up out of nowhere, like enchanting passersby who hop on only to tighten a screw, scrub off a stain, or shake the life out of us. They may be our unnoticeable young cousin at family dinners, the crazy neighbor everyone avoids, a stranger on the streets in a foreign country... or, in my case, a blast from the past.

THROUGH THICK AND THIN

As life progresses, challenges will pass, and doubt might creep in. You might find yourself questioning the very foundations of your existence. Amidst this chaos, turn to your steadfast support system and allow them to remind you of who you are.

Those will eagerly come forward without prompting, declaring their commitment to stand by your side. These are the people who become the pillars of your support system, ready to lend a helping hand and be an integral part of your triumphant narrative, and those are the people you keep in your backstage.

These people act like catalysts for your progress. Through their love, care, and enthusiasm toward you, they hold you accountable during your journey. They have the privilege to correct and reprimand you, telling you the blunt truth, shaking you away from any sugarcoating, and giving you the feedback that will propel you forward. They are next to us to hold us accountable for whatever journey we're going through.

Your support crew will tell you what you need rather than what you want to hear. They know you, with all your weaknesses and vulnerabilities, and will act as a nurturing space, applauding your endeavors.

As I mentioned, your crew isn't confined only to the people around you. This kind of support can be obtained from other sources. Writers motivate through their books, and artists inspire with their songs. You may find wisdom in literally every corner of the world.

Tip - The Reset Button

When familiarity begins to veil our eyes, nothing could be as refreshing as pressing the reset button and choosing to view things anew.

"I am devoted to surrounding myself with a faithful support crew."

Chapter Seven

Cast Your Actors
May the Auditions Begin

IN LIFE, WE OFTEN excel and achieve great things on our own. However, when it comes to big projects and causes that reach the world, we discover that collaboration with others is inevitable.

Thus, when the domino effect of my transformation built momentum, it was time for me to rearrange the people's rules in my life. Those who no longer fit were graciously released, moving to the sidelines as observers and sometimes even departing from my life entirely. Those destined to be part of my inner circle stayed close, either kept their roles or were reassigned to new ones, depending on what my essence wanted to do next. As some space cleared up, I searched for new people to invite into my life to bring my vision and dreams to fruition.

Drumroll...

In this Act, beloved Emiku, it is my utmost pleasure and honor to present your play's beloved actors to you!

"It takes two to tango."

DRAMATIS PERSONAE

ACT VII - SCENE 1

FOGS - fogs of the present, representing all that's making her vision blurry, distracting her from her true calling.

HER - a weak, desperate young woman.

SHADOWS - shadows of the past, representing all the memories haunting her, impeding her from going forward with her life.

SETTING

A lonely, faraway land.

TIME

One decade ago, after a turning point in her life forced her to face new challenges.

ACT VII

SCENE 1

SETTING: She's alone in a desolate foreign place. The atmosphere suffocates her with dense gloom. She stands in an empty void. Behind her, two sinister silhouettes stand, casting an ominous pall. They whisper doubts and fears, amplifying her isolation.

AT RISE: On center stage, she stands, her eyes fixed on the emptiness before her. Motionless. Her rapid breaths aggravate the stillness as she clings to her suitcase and tightly grasps a purse. A solitary white spotlight hovers just above her head, emphasizing the vulnerability on her face.

FOGS

(Sinister laugh)

(Walks forward towards HER, rubbing its hands together)

Welcome, welcome, welcome, well, not so much.

HER

(Not looking at it, eyes wide open)

Who are you?

FOGS

(Stands next to her, red spotlight on it)

I'm FOGS; I've been waiting for you. What took you so long?

HER

I don't understand. Do you know me?

FOGS

I do. I know your secrets, but they don't sit well with me. You're unwelcome here, believe it. The winds of change are blowing, demanding your departure. A storm is coming, and it will reshape everything you hold dear.

HER

What do you mean?

FOGS

(Mockingly)

So, I heard you're a singer and actress. Really? How self-indulgent of you! Flaunting yourself with your blond hair in front of millions, thinking you're so special. Have you no sense of decency? What a disgrace, having no regard for norms and values. What about your parents? You should be ashamed of your behavior.

HER

Art is my sanctuary, and I find solace and meaning in it. And I do have parents; their memory fuels my journey while I experienced their painful loss.

FOGS

Ah, an orphan. How pitiful. Pay attention to my words; if you wish for our coexistence, you shall bend to my will. I demand enormous alterations from you.

(Trying to show care and sympathy)

Believe me, it's for your own wretched sanity, my dear. Resistance shall only bring despair upon your soul.

SHADOWS

(Walks from behind, stands next to her, opposite to FOGS, a dark blue spotlight on it)

You're feeble; your weakness demands obedience. You're worthless, unable to survive without guidance. The words FOGS is whispering hold a twisted sense of reason. You shall abide by its advice. You've been stripped of all you held dear, isolated in your despair. You're alone; embrace this solitude, for you are truly alone, abandoned, and forsaken.

HER

What? Why should I listen to you?

SHADOWS

Because I'm you, I know what you need. I'm Shadows.

HER

Shadows?

SHADOWS

Yes, Shadows of your past. You brought me with you, remember?

HER

And you know who that is?

SHADOWS

Yes, it's FOGS, FOGS of the present.

(Sighs)

SHADOWS

You heard what FOGS said, comply. If you wanted to exist in this realm, you had to do what it said. I know you; I'm familiar with your essence. Every detail is memorized; you don't have what it takes to do what it says.

(Lights off over FOGS and SHADOWS)

HER

Yes, I confess, I am afraid. It seems like my artistic endeavors offer no solace in this desolation. What a reminder of my misguided choices. I'm desperate, and I can feel the peril waiting for me. Perhaps they were right all along. From this moment onward, I abandoned my identity; it has become a treacherous liability.

(BLACKOUT)

(END OF SCENE 1)

DRAMATIS PERSONAE

ACT VII - SCENE 2

HER - a messy, lost woman going through one of the toughest phases of her life.

MAN - a thirty-year-old man, an old friend of hers.

SETTING

On the street.

TIME

On a sunny day... about ten years ago.

ACT VII

SCENE 2

SETTING: a busy street basking in gentle sunshine, open stores create a vibrant activity. Fashion boutiques showcase stylish textures and colors. Sparkling jewelry displays mesmerize with their allure. A tantalizing aroma of freshly ground coffee beans drifts by from a café. The street radiates a thriving urban scene.

AT RISE: A father blows bubbles, bringing joy to his child, and two girls playfully jump rope nearby. An older man crosses the street holding his wife's hand, and a young boy on his bike exchanges pleasantries with the baker. There she stands, buying cotton candy from a kiosk. In a humorous twist, she bumps into a passing man.

HER

(Startled)

Excuse you! Watch where you're going.

MAN

(Offended)

It seems you believe the street is yours! Wake up to reality, ma'am! It's a bustling day; pay attention and be mindful of where you are.

HER

(Slowly realizing)

Wait, don't you recognize me?

MAN

(Disbelief)

What?

HER

It's me! Don't you remember me? We used to work together when we were young!

MAN

(Looks closely)

Remind me where? I don't think so.

HER

We have pictures together!

(She takes her phone and shows him a picture they took together long ago)

See! That's us!

MAN

This is me in the picture, but you seem very different from the woman in the picture with me.

HER

You're serious; why are you acting weird all of a sudden?

MAN

Ah! Now, I remember. You're the one acting weird, walking around like a faded, worn-out silhouette of a person, lacking all vibrancy.

HER

(Stands in silence)

MAN

(Interrupting, trying to end the conversation)

Can't you see the difference between you and the woman in the picture?

(Pauses)

We'll get to talk when you're YOU again.

(Walks away)

HER

(Stands in shock as she watches him walk away)

Wait!

(She notices a store window; she sees her reflection. She traces her face with both hands, resenting her tangled red, messy hair)

HER

I don't like my hair.

HER

(Looks down)

Since when did I start venturing out in pajamas? What are those? Flip-flops?

HER

(A look of disbelief accentuates her worn-out, weary face)

Whom have I become?

(BLACKOUT)

(END OF ACT VII)

THE UPGRADE

The breakthrough I experienced on the sandy shore in 2014 ignited in the depths of my being a never-ending refinement process that spread like an irreversible ripple effect into all the areas of my life. And as the ins and knobs of my character puzzle got reshaped, the connections and relationships that involved me faced one of two fates. Those that morphed along sustained our compatibility and allowed our collaboration to blossom. While those who didn't wither and fell off my twigs like leaves and spoiled fruits no longer resonated with the taste of the essence.

It all started to happen when I began to change people's positions in my life. Those meant to stay on my stage remained, and those who didn't fit were thankfully released and sent to the audience, and sometimes totally outside the theater. The people who still wanted to attend the show but weren't invited by me were granted random seats. Yet the people I invited myself had the right to meet me privately backstage before the show began. Only those who resonated with me were welcome to join and witness my victorious endeavors.

Emiku, allow me to bring you an example. If your story narrates the discovery of your soul mate and your heart burns with happiness and purpose to live joyfully, the first step is to announce an open audition. This call will welcome the right person into your life and let the world know who is invited and embraced to partake in this beautiful journey. To conduct a successful audition, it's essential to precisely define the character you seek, ensuring a perfect fit for the role. We can discover individuals who resonate with our shared value system by doing so.

Hence, the life director's crucial task is to ensure the casting of the right actors who embody the essence of the story. Not everyone can play any role; even highly skilled individuals may not always be the perfect fit. In such cases, they could be considered for a future chapter, preserving the narrative's authenticity.

And what if two individuals fit the same role? Who do I choose? You might ask, Emiku. Well, I'd say, trust your heart.

THE SOLOIST

Monologues are beautiful and unique in their own way. And sometimes, they are very powerful, too. Like solo performances, they put the musician or the actor alone under the spotlight and highlight their skill, talent, beauty, and magic. And when the audience applauds, all the glory goes to that one person performing center stage.

However, most stories require an entire cast of coherent actors to represent all the characters and facets of the plot. Similarly, most musical pieces require two or more synced musicians to play the different instruments, sounds, and notes written in the score sheet.

Similarly, your life is not a solo performance or a one-person show, sweet Emiku, nor is it a single life-long monologue. Imagine how boring, dull, and even pointless such a life could be. You are here on earth as an essential, irreplaceable character in the Play of Life. And your own life play cannot exist without the priceless presence of the other actors and your invaluable interactions with them. Your show will become dysfunctional and unappealing in the long run without them.

When totally alone, the play becomes a solo act, a Monologue... However, in a story where the character interacts with other characters, the number of roles a character plays in a story reflects the number of relationships they have.

A CELLIST IN THE ORCHESTRA

We are not only to perform within the same genre but also play the exact same piece of music. Our roles in life are intricately defined by the diverse types of relationships we hold. While all of them involve connections, being a sibling, a child, a mother, or a partner, each entails distinct roles and responsibilities. Likewise, in a professional setting, being an employee differs significantly from being a coworker or a boss. Our roles constantly evolve based on the type and nature of our relationships, as we may move away from certain people who no longer connect with us or resonate with our values.

UNSUPPORTIVE ACTORS

Just as a tree's physical environment influences its growth and health, so does its biological environment, which includes the animals that eat from it and find shelter in it, as well as other plants, insects, and microorganisms. Similarly, the other characters in your story greatly influence the growth and expression of your character's essence in the Play of Life.

Some biotic factors in the tree's ecosystem may hinder its growth or even severely damage it, such as some rodents, insects, fungi, and parasites. The same is true for the types of characters in your story and the quality of the actors you employ to play their roles.

The first step necessary in such a case is to eliminate these harmful factors by building fences, traps, or using insecticides... Similarly, when the harmony and progression of your story are hampered by the involvement of unfitting characters or actors, the first step necessary is to rewrite the profiles of your story's characters and send the inadequate actors away in love and gratitude.

END OF CONTRACT

Pay attention to your body now, Emiku, and adjust your posture until your bones feel comfortable. Straighten your spine and stick out your chin, Emiku, for you are about to play a majestic role. With your eyes wide open, visualize your seat transforming into a deluxe personalized director's chair. The words "Emiku, The Life Director" starkly contrast its black back panel. You have come so far. Feel your greatness building up in your muscles. Feel your grandeur, your value, your power.

The room is getting dimmer. You are in an old cinema. To your right stands an old film projector. You are in the control room. As you turn on the projector, you hear different yet familiar sounds. You totally love this. And now you hear a loud and sweet beep as a circle with a thin black number 5 in its middle appears on the wall across the room. Another beep, 4. You smile with anticipation. Beep, 3. Feel your excitement rising. Beep, 2. You know what's coming. Beep, 1. Close your eyes.

Different scenes are streaming one after the other. You recognize them. They are scenes from your past and present life, but you are not in them. The shots are focused solely on the other actors, following them as they play their diverse roles in your story. It's evaluation time. Take your time contemplating and studying these performances. How satisfied are you with this show?

Tip – Objectivity

Try not to take things personally, as this will never serve you. Instead, focus on extracting all the positive feedback you can find in any situation.

Tip – Love and Gratitude

Remember that every person in your life is playing a role. Instead of feeling resentment, grudge, or hate, send them love and thank them for helping you become the great person you are today.

THE AUDITIONS

In theater, casting directors want to see that the actor knows his art. Body movements, facial expressions, tone of voice, smooth transitions, vocal strength, stage presence, character confidence, and the ability to portray the role given are all embedded in the sense of professionalism that casting directors want to see.

They look for professionalism, talent, skill, a courteous relationship with other production members, creativity, the ability to interpret and perform roles creatively, being a source of inspiration, a good attitude, and physical attributes.

As the casting director of your own life, what attributes and traits are you looking for? Which parts or aspects are most important to you?

COLLABORATORS

While some biotic factors in the tree's ecosystem may be harmful or even deadly, other factors are beneficial and sometimes even essential for its survival and growth. After all, a fruit tree is part of an entire ecosystem. Not only does it play a role in feeding the living creatures around it, but it also sometimes depends on them for growth, such as in the case of insect pollinators like beetles, ants, and bees.

Thus, you must not only send away the people who no longer serve your story but also audition and cast those necessary for advancing and embellishing your life show.

SCRIPTS FOR THE ACTORS

Adjust your posture and stick out your chin again, Emiku, for you are again in your personalized director's chair. Notice the texture and volume of your essence's power invigorating your cells.

The room is getting dimmer. You are in the old cinema again. However, this time, across the room hangs a huge banner over a wooden platform. It reads "Emiku's Next Life Chapter - Acting Auditions". You hear distant, unintelligible chatter. Actors of all ages, colors, shapes, and experiences are lined up in the lobby, waiting for you to open the doors. On the table before, you lay the scripts of the different characters in your story, which these contestants hope to get.

You take the first file and flip through its pages. All the papers are blank; the same goes for the other files. The auditions are about to start, yet you're unsure what you want since your empty scripts offer no guidance. Regaining awareness of the chair you're sitting in, you close your eyes and remember who you are. You are the director and scriptwriter of your own life.

Breathe in, filling your lungs with the essence of your next life chapter. Breathe out, feeling firm, strong, and secure in your body. Revive the images of your next life chapter and immerse yourself in them. Remember every detail, every experience you seek to develop, and all the emotions that you desire to feel. Then think of all the things that you are patiently waiting to share with your actors, as well as how you will serve them and collaborate and co-create with them... And now, focus on the actors themselves.

Whom would you like to cast for your play? Whom will you choose?

Tip – Pleasure

Any exercise could be fun and freeing. Focus on finding joy, and you shall find it.

Tip – Trust

Our beliefs and thoughts micromanage our life and create it. Trust that what serves you always finds its way to you, and it shall find it indeed.

"I am devoted to the appreciation and constant evaluation of my actors."

Chapter Eight

Rehearse

Practice Makes Perfect

I WAS IN A hurry, putting on whatever, singing without a warmup, forgetting lines... I was holding enormous bags of knowledge that wouldn't mean a thing if there was no actual practice of any of it. And as you leave a tree unpruned and do not take the new car you just bought on trial rides, you'll never be able to find where the lacks reside.

Repetitively practicing a skill until it becomes second nature, like an actor creating a new story and character, is essential for mastering our roles in life. Rehearsing these roles allows us to perform effortlessly, without fear of forgetting lines, and empowers us to improvise when necessary. Through dedication and rehearsal, we transform our roles into a natural and confident expression of ourselves, perfecting our script and performance in the best way possible.

Before unveiling my method in this book, I invested time rehearsing, practicing, and working with various individuals. As a conclusive step, I conducted a real-life workshop with actual participants to thoroughly test and experiment with this knowledge. The valuable insights gained from this hands-on experience ensured the method's effectiveness and readiness for sharing with a wider audience.

Drumroll...

In this Act, Emiku, it is my utmost pleasure and honor to present the fine-tuned embodiment of your essence!

"In the dance of mastery, step by step, skills become adept."

DRAMATIS PERSONAE

ACT VIII - SCENE 1

HER - a worn-out young lady, barely able to move.

NARRATOR - a voice describing her actions.

SETTING

In her room.

TIME

This scene occurs when she is disconnected from what she knows and the practical level of her knowledge.

ACT VIII

SCENE 1

SETTING: A dark room with a grey bed takes center stage. Nothing else is around it.

AT RISE: SHE lies in bed, hands crossed over her stomach. SHE looks at the ceiling.

HER

(Sighs)

Dreams are hovering over my brain. Each cell is showered with an aromatic desire that I wish to embody. My being feels the urge to overflow.

(Small boxes descend from above, each one is of a different color. A twinkling sound emerges. The boxes are very charming and sparkly, they stop mid-air, a bit out of her reach)

HER

(SHE stretches her right hand, trying to reach one of them. SHE fails. SHE tries with her left hand. It's pointless. SHE gets up and tries again. SHE fails again. But SHE notices something unusual about these boxes: each one has a note written on its bottom side)

HER (cont.)

(Reading off of one of the notes)

So you could reach me and make me see the light, you'll have to sing along with my melodies.

(Suddenly, a symphony emerges, SHE's surprised)

HER

(Vocalizes, SHE's out of tune. SHE hasn't been practicing her vocal sessions well)

(The box ascends farther than where it originally was)

HER

(Tries to read the bottom of another box)

So you could feel my physical presence and unravel my treasures, you'll have to get the dancer out of your system.

(That's when classical music abruptly starts playing, pushing her to sway along. SHE starts moving along. SHE doesn't do a good job. Her legs are frail; SHE hasn't been working out. Her arms are not in harmony. Her neck is stiff. Her shoulders are locked. SHE forgot to stretch in the past couple of months)

HER

(Wondering)

What's going on with me?

(The box is farther now as SHE fails to check the task)

HER

(Jumps on the bed again, and SHE's tired. SHE gets on the tips of her toes trying to read the note on a third hanging box)

As actors unveil their talents, acting out feelings that are not their own, you'll have to embody emotions upon your face, going through different states as the music guides you. Excel, and you'll own what I have for you.

HER

(As the music starts, SHE hears a suspenseful melody, and SHE tries to get out emotions of terror and fear. SHE fails. The music shifts to a melancholic symphony, and SHE tries to shed a tear. SHE absolutely cannot. It's been so long)

(By then, all the boxes will ascend and disappear. SHE failed to reach any of them)

HER (cont.)

Why is this happening to me? I feel...

NARRATOR

SHE finds herself at a loss for words, not in the sense that she doesn't know what to say, but rather an inability to utter a single sound.

HER

(Sits on the bed, her hands on her neck)

Words escape her memory as if the script of her own play has vanished into thin air. Sitting in disbelief, she ponders the mysterious forces at play. Could it be that her lofty expectations led her to believe that the boxes might come to the palm of her hand? She tried to reach them, but it didn't work. In truth, she hadn't been singing or dancing much.

HER

(Lays on the bed in sadness)

(Deep down, she believed that she possessed all the qualities within her, assuming that things would naturally align. There must be an essential ingredient that she has yet to discover)

(BLACKOUT)

(END OF SCENE 1)

DRAMATIS PERSONAE

ACT VIII - SCENE 2

HER - an enthusiastic young lady.

NARRATOR - a voice describing her movements.

SETTING

In her room, then the scene shifts to a huge stage. An imaginary scene takes place in her mind.

TIME

This scene is out of space and time, representing all the times she rehearsed and experimented with her knowledge.

ACT VIII

SCENE 2

SETTING: A bed is on the center stage, with drawers to its right and a closet to its left. A pretty red rug lies next to it. A mirror stands next to the drawers.

AT RISE: SHE sits on the bed, some jazzy music playing while SHE scrolls on her computer. It's just another night.

HER

(Sighs in surprise)

I can't believe this!

(Reads what's on-screen out loud in a very quick way)

A one-time opportunity unfolds as the doors of the grand theater open once more, unveiling a slot for a dazzling one-hour performance. Do you possess the brilliance and flair to seize the stage?

Waste no time; reach out to us, secure your place, and own this once-in-a-lifetime chance for triumph.

HER

(Overwhelmed, picks up her phone and dials a number)

Hello? I'm taking the spot available on the grand theater's reopening!

(Takes a pause, listening to what's said over the phone)

HER (cont.)

Yes, I do! I'm a performer, and I'll give the audience the show they came to see. Check my work online, and you'll see what I'm talking about. Great, I'll wait for your answer.

(SHE puts the phone down; SHE's barely able to take a breath in as the phone rings again)

HER

Hello?

(Shouts in disbelief)

Really? I'll be there!

NARRATOR (VO)

(Upbeat music starts)

That's where it all started; a deadline is approaching. She only has less than a month to get everything in place.

(SHE jumps out of bed; the drawer and mirror are swept to the right, while the bed and closet are swept to the left alongside the rug. The stage is clear)

HER

(SHE dances in sync with the melodic rhythmic music, tirelessly rehearsing, pouring her heart and soul into every aspect of the performance. SHE moves from one corner to another so eloquently, starting with fragile small steps, transforming into bigger leaps, stronger steps, with a more certain pace)

NARRATOR (VO)

Late into the night, the sound of her vibrant voice filled the air as she engaged in vocal sessions, crushing obstacles, overcoming stuck fears, and conquering new territories of herself.

HER

(During the NARRATOR's description, SHE starts doing physical workouts, stretching every muscle in her body, flexing her neck, straightening her back, and adjusting her posture. SHE vocalizes in front of her teacher, who applauds her. When the NARRATOR finishes, SHE leaves the stage)

NARRATOR (VO)

It's the big day.

(Yellow lights shower on the stage. Four men drag four Greek pillars and place them in the background. A full orchestra enters and forms a semi-circle in front of the columns. SHE enters in a golden dress)

NARRATOR (VO cont.)

There she is, a living, breathing testament of an unwavering, dedicated spirit. That night, she danced passionately, and a flawless representation of her character was seen. She captivated hearts. Her voice soared through the rows in front of her, echoed by tears and screams of joy from the audience. As the final notes of her performance resonated, she stood on that stage, her dream realized, and her efforts were rewarded.

HER

(She stands in pride, her arms wide open, and takes in all the love and appreciation the audience is giving her. SHE whispers to herself)

This is exactly how I imagined it to be.

(SHE hugs herself)

NARRATOR (VO)

For the first time in many years, she felt as if she were behind a telescope, gazing at the night sky and observing far-fetched galaxies that had once been blurry. And now, with only a minuscule adjustment of the telescope's lens, the image was finally clear.

(BLACKOUT)

(END OF ACT VIII)

RANDOM BREEDS RANDOM

Listen to this story, Emiku. Years ago, I found myself at a fancy and glamorous event, though I was going through a tough phase in my life. The demands of that period left me with little time for my daily vocal practice and stretching, which affected my performance abilities. Consequently, I chose not to perform during that time.

However, at that event, I was accompanied by my family and a group of friends, including an organizer who happened to be a friend of mine. Upon spotting me, they urged me to sing just one song of my choice. Reluctantly, I agreed to their request and took the stage.

When I started singing, the crowd erupted in cheers, showing their support. Yet, I knew deep down that my performance wasn't up to my usual standards. Due to my lack of practice and flexibility, I tried to avoid the high notes to prevent injuries. While the audience enjoyed the performance and lifted their spirits, I couldn't help but criticize myself from a professional perspective. I knew I would have never allowed myself to perform under such limitations under normal circumstances.

When we don't rehearse, our outcomes will be inconsistent, incoherent, random, and arbitrary. And while sometimes they might even be undesired and paradoxical, at other times, they might be misleading and totally out of sync with who we are and what we aim to do.

We need to rehearse to secure the outcomes we want, fight self-doubt, remove obstacles that might hinder our progress, and communicate the newest version of our character to the world clearly and confidently.

SECOND NATURE

Rehearsing the embodiment of your newness enough times allows it to become second nature.

Rehearsals can be likened to the scientific method applied to the art of performance. Just as scientists conduct experiments to test hypotheses and refine their theories, performers use rehearsals to explore and refine their artistic expression. By doing so, they can unlock new dimensions of creativity and deliver truly captivating experiences to their audiences.

Rehearsals offer a unique space for performers to experiment, take risks, and discover hidden nuances within their craft. They allow pushing boundaries, challenging assumptions, and exploring alternative interpretations. Through this process, performers can uncover fresh perspectives and unique artistic choices that may have otherwise remained untapped.

Moreover, rehearsals serve as a bridge between the individual artist and the collective ensemble. They foster a sense of camaraderie, collaboration, and shared purpose among performers. By working together in rehearsals, artists can synchronize their efforts, synchronize their movements, and fine-tune their interactions. This collective synergy elevates the overall quality of the performance and creates a cohesive and harmonious experience for the audience.

Rehearsals also allow performers to develop a deep understanding of their material. By repeatedly practicing and refining their skills, they become intimately familiar with every performance aspect, whether memorizing lines, mastering complex choreography, or perfecting musical phrasing. This level of mastery instills confidence, enabling performers to deliver their best even in high-pressure situations.

Additionally, rehearsals provide a controlled environment for troubleshooting and problem-solving. They offer an opportunity to identify and address potential pitfalls, technical challenges, or logistical issues before they occur during an actual performance. By proactively tackling these obstacles, performers can ensure a seamless and flawless execution when the spotlight is on.

In essence, rehearsals are a mere repetition of what has already been established and a fertile ground for artistic exploration, collaboration, mastery, and innovation. They empower performers to transcend boundaries, refine their skills, and deliver truly transformative performances for themselves and their audiences.

TESTED AND CERTIFIED

When a professional and efficient farmer seeks to harvest specific high-quality fruits, they don't take unlabeled seeds from unknown origins and plant them randomly in unmonitored environments. Rather, they search for the best-certified seeds available on the market. As their adjective suggests, certified seeds are good-quality seeds officially recognized to have passed several tests that ensure they meet specific standards. Planting such seeds allows the farmer to have good expectations of the quantity and quality of the harvest.

After hand-picking their seeds, they carefully plant them according to the instructions on their packets, using their knowledge and years of practice. Then, they invest their time and energy in growing them and caring for them closely until they yield their desired harvest, and they may keep doing so for years to reap the same fruits.

For best results, use the right amounts of water, the right soil, the right exposure to light, and whether direct or indirect... Thus, continuous diligent care for the plant is as important in determining the quality of the fruits as the quality of the seed itself. What differentiates a professional and efficient farmer from others is the experience they accumulate by repeatedly taking care of their fruit tree.

Just as random measures don't yield specific outcomes, living your days randomly will hardly ever get you where you want to get. Reaping the fruits of your essence doesn't merely depend on the quality of your essence alone but on thoughtful and intentional rehearsal.

Similarly, to reach the fullness of your potential, the embodiment of your essence requires tailor-made individualized steps that will get you from where you are now and bridge the gap between you right now and the desired outcome you want to achieve...

What do you need to rehearse to achieve your life's Next Chapter? Do you need to become more knowledgeable, patient, skilled, fitter, or healthier? What would make you thrive? Rehearse, try again and again; what is your right soil? The right amount of sun? What do you need to perfect? Clothes? Words? Lines? Attitude? Body language? Facial expressions?

THE MONOLOGUE

Imagine yourself standing on a glorious stage right under the spotlight. You are wearing the right outfit, the props are in place, the stage is set. All is in place. In your hands, you're holding a script, a monologue. You are about to present your refined character to the world.

Other directors are auditioning you. You have this one time, one opportunity, one chance to prove your authentic embodiment versus that poor, fake, and empty performance. The Directors of Life of the

World search for genuine, authentic, and original people. Life wants to recruit actors, doers, and contributors who are not ashamed to be themselves, who own up to their powers, who know who they are, and who are willing to go a long way to defend their vision and fulfill their mission... People who want to serve, love, PLAY...

Tip - Bold and Courageous
In this one life, you have nothing to lose except yourself. So stand your ground and raise your head high!

IN THE THICK OF IT

As I told you before, dear Emiku, I had to practice every step of this book to take birth. It took me years and years of breaks so I could bring together my broken and lost pieces. That was the first step. I had to rehearse all my knowledge, embodying it by doing the things that I loved and yearned to accomplish years ago. It wasn't before 2019 that I published my first album, which I fully wrote myself.

Then, as a second step of rehearsals and practice, I experimented with this method among my friends and family. Those individuals helped me make tweaks here and there to enhance further and embellish this modality.

Finally, as a closing testimony of my tireless journey of experimentation, I created a workshop to fully grasp this method and bestow it upon individuals who were total strangers. That's when I realized that I was finally ready to pursue the writing process of this book and eventually advertise it.

Allow me to share this story with you, Emiku. Once, I was set to portray a younger, skilled Latin dancer in a musical video. In front of the mirror, I rehearsed my lines and dance steps, experimenting with different outfits while perfecting my voice and the lyrics.

The script for my video clip was complete. Daily workouts became essential as I strived to embody the character authentically. The dress was chosen, and I meticulously prepared it with hair and makeup tailored for filming. Everything was set for the shoot—the location, props, lights, crew, and supporting actors—all ready to bring the project to life. With the director, videographer, and my dance partner in sync, we were poised for a captivating performance.

The day of the shooting approached swiftly, and the process was challenging. Hours of workouts, dance practices, stretching, and vocal rehearsals demanded perseverance.

Yet, what fueled my determination, Emiku, was my unwavering love and passion for the project. It was a dream that enveloped me every night, so real and tangible that it materialized a month before its actual realization. My dedication and devotion turned my vision into a beautiful reality.

ADJUSTING THE LENS 101

Metaphorically, "adjusting the lens" is usually used to describe standing in a different position to have a different perception of a situation or issue. It signifies a shift in focus or a new way of seeing things.

Adjusting the lens allows you to gain a new perspective by consciously changing how you view a situation, problem, or concept, which may require considering different angles, exploring alternative viewpoints, or adopting a more open-minded approach.

Adjusting the lens would greatly benefit from adapting to new information, as new information or insights become available, adjusting the lens involves incorporating this knowledge and adjusting one's understanding or interpretation accordingly.

Adjusting the lens sometimes also invites you to shift your focus regarding your priorities by changing the emphasis or importance placed on certain aspects. It may involve refocusing attention on different elements or recognizing different aspects that were previously overlooked.

Essentially, adjusting the lens is about being flexible, open to new ideas, and willing to modify one's perspective or approach in light of changing circumstances or information.

What Do They See?

Ask your support crew to sit in the audience, then chat sincerely with them.

How well do you handle criticism?

In which ways was their feedback constructive?

What are some practical steps or sets of actions that they recommended?

Tip - Feedback

Feedback, whether positive or negative, can serve as a great mirror. Failure is just feedback, too.

Whether you make it clear to them or not, try to gather feedback from your supporting actors.

*How pleasurable is it to play
with me?*

*What would my fellow actors
appreciate?*

*How predictable am I? In which
ways is this positive?*

For extra input, you may seek out a stranger to grasp an outsider's perspective.

*What impressions do others
have about me?*

*What are some recurring pat-
terns?*

ADJUSTING THE LENS 201

In photography, "adjusting the lens" refers to changing the camera lens settings to achieve the desired photographic outcome. Adjusting the lens may involve either manually or automatically setting the focus distance to ensure the subject is clear and well-defined, adjusting the aperture, zooming in or out, activating or deactivating the image stabilization, and using filters to enhance colors, reduce glare, add special effects, or achieve other desired visual effects. By adjusting the lens settings, photographers can control the focus, depth of field, exposure, and other parameters to capture the image they envision.

While photographers work on adjusting the lens, actors work on fine-tuning their own embodiment of the character, aiming to become a fully realized three-dimensional character. Bring the character to life, embody the character, and adjust your real-life, real-time representation until it becomes identical to the image you have in mind...

The art of acting rests upon the transformative power of rehearsal. In this sacred realm, we commit our lines to memory and immerse ourselves in the essence of our characters through relentless repetition and a relentless pursuit of authenticity.

Train your muscles, practice your lines, rehearse your steps, cut your hair or leave it to grow, add a few calories to your diet, or cut them... Are you truly the person in the poster?

WHAT DO I SEE?

Dear Emiku, you might want to take a video of yourself presenting your monologue. Sit in the audience, watch yourself from an outsider's perspective, and try to answer these questions as neutrally and objectively as possible.

What needs to be tweaked about
your performance?

Are you coming off strange?

How well do your words convey
what you mean to say?

How coherent is your behavior
with your values?

What is still missing?

Finally, please sit in the director's chair, my dear, and watch yourself generate positive feedback.

Tip – Critic Not Allowed

You are your Life Director, not a critic. Life is a Play, and you are merely finetuning the embodiment of your character's essence.

"I am devoted to the relentless rehearsal of my essence's expressions."

Chapter Nine

Advertise Yourself
Show the World Who You Are

NO SHINY, DAZZLING THING would matter if no eyes could witness its light. The same goes for us. The importance of our own self-expression is immense, for without it, we would stay invisible, unnoticed, and unable to proceed with our endeavors.

Drumroll...

In this Act, Emiku, it is my utmost pleasure and honor to present the advertisement campaign of your essence to you!

"What is beauty without its beholder? What is a rare wine without a connoisseur? What are cultures without their artifacts? What's an awakening without its impacts? Who is Shakespeare without Romeo and Juliet? What good is a fruit rotting in a basket? What good is great wisdom when forgotten? What good is a treasure that is locked and hidden?"

DRAMATIS PERSONAE

ACT IX - SCENE 1

HEAD - her mind playing the role of her inner critic.

HER - a distracted woman, too insecure and vulnerable.

NEIGHBOR - her neighbor, a woman on the new street she lives on.

SETTING

In her house.

TIME

About a decade ago, from our present day.

ACT IX

SCENE 1

SETTING: In her home, the living room is a scene of disorder. Toys scatter the floor. Dust particles twinkle like crystals, illuminated by the sun's rays streaming through the windows. Resting on the small table, two dirty glasses. The TV flickers in the background. Plates from today's lunch remain abandoned on the dining table. Amidst this disarray, a vibrant orange couch takes center stage while a serene green armchair stands to its left.

AT RISE: she diligently tidies up the surroundings, and a female character finds respite on the couch. It's her (HEAD). Her legs are elegantly crossed as she meticulously tends to her nails. A palpable sense of discontent hangs in the air as if everything is unraveling and spiraling downward.

HEAD

(Shouting)

Clean this place up; this is unbearable.

HER

(Grunts)

I hate this!

HEAD

Come on! It's like we're living in a dumpster; I can't believe this.

HER

(Ties her messy red hair in a bun, takes a broom, starts cleaning the floor)

HEAD

You're such a mess.

(Looks at the door, startled)

Huh! Cheer up, someone's coming; take your antidepressant right now!

HEAD (cont.)

(Sarcastic)

Try the whole pack; I doubt it'll help anyway.

HER

It's not the time for it yet.

(Doorbell rings, she opens the door, a woman appears in a yellow summer dress, holding a small bag)

NEIGHBOR

Hello, welcome to the neighborhood! This is for you.

(Hands her the bag)

HEAD

(Impatiently)

Damn it, you're a mess, take it from her and thank her... Look alive!

HER

Thank you, come in, please.

NEIGHBOR

(Steps in)

Thank you, but I can't stay for too long, so do you like it here?

HER

I love the area

HEAD

(Interrupts her)

Don't you say anything about the museums and art centers.

HER

(Whispering)

I know.

(Continues normally)

It's lovely, the schools are good for the kids, and many playing areas exist.

HEAD

Good, now show her you have a stable, old-fashioned, NOR-MAL-UNCRAZY life.

NEIGHBOR

Ah, wonderful, so what do you do for a living?

HEAD

(Abruptly)

Education.

HER

I'm an educator.

NEIGHBOR

Okay, and do you have any free time?

HEAD

(Interrupts)

Housework.

HER

(Looks at MIND, unamused)

I take care of my family. I'm a mother of two. I cook in the morning and clean up in the afternoon.

NEIGHBOR

(Excited)

You should come with me and my friends to the new club down the street, you'll love the vibe, and we're so much fun!

HEAD

(Startled)

Never! If you don't do well in such situations, they'll think you're a weirdo, so say no.

HER

(Hesitant)

I wish... but I don't have time

NEIGHBOR

Sad, it's fine. I'll head out now and see you around. Thanks for having me.

(Leaves the stage)

(HEAD stands near HER)

HEAD

You did well, surprisingly.

HER

Did I?

HEAD

(Sighs)

As long as you're not talking about your artistic endeavors, you'll be fine. I can't handle any more headaches, well... me-aches.

HER

But I want to go out sometime.

HEAD

Don't you dare say that you know what you want? They'll laugh at you, no one will take you seriously, and they'll say you're messed up.

HER

Yeah, I know, no one has to know that I love singing; I'll show them only what they want to see.

HEAD

Exactly, and please take that pill. I'm exhausted.

(Exits the stage)

HER

(Her body succumbs to the weight of sorrow; she traverses the living room, clutching a pill in her hand, gazing upon it, and sighs wearily, a lament for the words left unspoken, the truths about her own existence. With a firm resolve, she consumes the pill, slurping down the depth of what was unwelcome about her)

(BLACKOUT)

(END OF SCENE 1)

DRAMATIS PERSONAE

ACT IX - SCENE 2

HOST - a middle-aged woman interviewing her.

HER - a successful, inspirational woman.

SETTING

On the stage of a talk show.

TIME

This scene is imaginary; it's a cumulative of all the times she appeared in interviews, podcasts, and TV shows.

ACT IX

SCENE 2

SETTING: A huge scene is set in the theater. Two purple one-seaters face each other center stage. A screen stands behind them. Two green plants are placed next to the left chair, and a coffee table is in the middle.

AT RISE: SHE sits to the right. The lights are on her, and facing her is a female host. Both of them are well-dressed. It's an international TV show.

(Generic music plays while the audience applauds)

HOST

(Announces joyfully)

Welcome back, everybody. We've finally reached our last segment for today. I know it's been so long since we've all been waiting for it, but here we are with Nadine Chammas!

(Audience applauds and cheers)

HER

(laughs)

Thank you so much for having me.

HOST

Nadine, you're here for one reason: to tell the world about your upcoming event. But first, please tell the world a bit about yourself.

HER

I'm Nadine, a mother, a wife, an artist.

I'm an inspiration, a sensation.

I'm an entertainer and a showwoman.

I'm empowering and supportive, and I overflow with positivity.

I'm the life director.

(Audience cheers)

HOST

What an extraordinary soul you are. And what will you be presenting in your show?

HER

This show will be one of a kind.

Music will play like never before.

I'll be performing my own songs throughout the event.

Visuals will be everywhere.

Interactive bits will take place.

It's pure entertainment and engagement.

HOST

That's amazing; I honestly can't wait for it. Such heart-warming and meticulously tailored events usually become a turning point in many people's lives. Is there anything you have in mind for this idea? What will the fans and the audience experience during your show?

HER

Well, in any event, people attend and leave.

They feel happy and energetic for a moment.

And then that's it, and it goes unnoticed.

But I aim for a life-changing experience like I always do.

For everyone who's attending or who hasn't yet decided to go.

Expect a deep experience, emotions flying here and there.

For in every song, there's a part of me.

In every corner, there's a chunk of Nadine.

Healing will take place.

Tears will flow, cleansing parts that no one knew existed.

People will feel present.

The past is long gone, and the future is far from one's reach.

The show is an opportunity to grasp the weight of the moment and savor it to its last drip.

HOST

No one doubts that, and we're all excited to see you there, performing for the first time internationally. Nadine, one last favor I'd like to ask.

(Points to a corner in front of NADINE)

HOST (cont.)

Looking at your camera over there, you have one minute to say whatever you feel like to our lovely audience.

HER

(Adjusts her position and looks at the camera)

To all the people who've been through a lot.

And to all the people who are still struggling.

Have faith in yourself.

You've got it all in you.

I've been there, and I'm still here.

And I'm here to tell you that it's fine.

Embrace whatever you have, accept it, and dance with it.

Let's all meet on the day of the event.

Let's celebrate pain, joy, journeys.

Let's celebrate life together.

Save the date, and I can't wait to see you all.

(BLACKOUT)

(END OF ACT IX)

VOICELESS VOICE

After gloriously retrieving my voice from the depths of the Mediterranean Sea like a long-lost treasure buried in the distant ocean floor, I did the unthinkable. I buried it in my chest.

My rhymes were trapped in the pages of my notebook, and my voice was suppressed in my chest like an abundant treasure buried on the ocean floor. My voice was like a pirate's hidden treasure chest for many years. What's the value of a chest lying kilometers below the surface, on the distant floor of the ocean?

I was singing in my pink room, but my only audience was my faithful pink walls. The only readers of my poems were the lines in my notebook. Though I had a voice, I was effectively voiceless. When I didn't share my opinion and chose silence, my isolation grew.

This book you're holding is put away in a dusty basement.... It amounts to nothing; haven't you been reading it?

I can remember literally all the times when I chose not to express who I truly was and what I really was doing for a living. In any social setting, either where I was sitting with only one person or even a group of people, the conversation would go in a pattern that I got used to eventually; they ask me what I did for a living, and after a quick assessment that I used to run in my brain, I'd reply in a way that would please the audience listening to me. I can't recall when I told you what I used to do.

I've always been a singer and songwriter, an actress and director, an inspirational woman, a positive parenting precursor, an entrepreneur, and a businesswoman. And to confess that I did all that while being a wife and a mother of two made me feel like a fraud in front of whoever lent me an ear.

But little did I know the amount of opportunities I missed by simply not expressing and describing myself bluntly in the open air. I was simply afraid of judgment and misperception; I was called "odd" for as long as I can remember.

ABSENT PRESENCE

Humanity created the alphabet, engravings, poetry, stories, and symbols to transfer knowledge and wisdom and communicate. Scholars define prehistory as events that occurred before written records existed in a given culture or society. History refers to the period after the invention of written records in a given culture or society. If you don't leave an imprint, it's like you never existed... Who would Shakespeare be if his plays were not recorded and preserved?

As teenagers in love, we used to write our names on school tables, engrave them on trees, sign them on walls... Take all your magic in right now, feel how deeply in love with it you are, and imagine all this work you've done going to waste like an immaculate fruit rotting on a shelf. Are you communicating your existence to the people around you? Do people around you know that you exist? Do they know what you have to offer? Are you present? And I'm not asking if you are aware, rather if you are really here... Are you showing yourself? Are you speaking up?

THE MISSING PIECE

All the disks need to be connected and working for a clock to work. If one wheel is missing, then the clock is non-functional. The same is true about Life. When you're not playing your roles, the play of life is missing one of its characters. When you hide away like a buried treasure chest, you selfishly deny the world the beauty and richness of your essence and impede the play of life from moving as it should. When you are dormant, parts of the people around you and life are also dormant.

Otherwise, these roles are pending and dormant like I was dormant (there is no story if the sleeping beauty remained in a deep sleep, time froze, and the entire kingdom was in deep slumber). All the disks need to be connected and working for a clock to work. If you remove a tree from its place, the animals and insects feeding on its fruits will have to migrate... the ecosystem will be broken... it might collapse.

And your lack of presence, absence in your ecosystems, in your plays is impeding the plays from happening... you not playing your role is impeding other people from playing their role, it's an act of service, it's you giving yourself because the play of life needs you to get going.

No one will know if you don't tell people you're here. You need to tell people you're here and advertise yourself. People out there are waiting for you; they need you. They've been calling your name... and life has been calling your name! Emiku! It's your turn!

FRUITLESS FRUITS

A tree advertises itself by its colors, leaves, and fruits' vibrancy. You can know a tree from how it looks, its health from the steadiness of its trunk, and the thickness of its wood... Yet, if a fruit tree is not harvested, it eventually dies.

A fruit tree is part of an ecosystem. Just as it takes nutrients from the soil, which the entire ecosystem contributes to, a fruit tree contributes to the ecosystem by offering its fruits for consumption by the animals and insects that need them... If you remove a tree from its place, the animals and insects feeding on its fruits will have to migrate..., and the ecosystem will be broken... it might collapse.

Imagine a fruit tree full of branches planted in a closed-off backyard that is fenced. There is no public access or service. The fruits fall on the ground and risk causing infections, which might eventually kill the tree.

That's to say, without advertisement, all yielded fruits are going to waste; no one benefits from them and their nutrients, no animal eats from them, and no one knows that you exist, that you worked so hard on yourself and rehearsed your magic well. No one will be able to collaborate with you or be entertained by your show...

MARKET RESEARCH SIMULATION

Imagine yourself standing on your dream stage. The house is empty. You are about to present a free show, the monologue you wrote in the previous chapter. The curtains are still closed, and you are peeking from behind them. You can see people of all shapes and forms entering the place and taking seats. Some of them are familiar, and some are total strangers. Some of them are coming in groups. Some others are coming alone. Some are choosing the farthest seats at the rear back end, and some are trying to negotiate over the front row seats... Some are hushing, trying to maintain order and silence, while others are already critiquing the place.

The lights go off, and the curtains open. There you are, standing center stage, right under the bright spotlight. Notice these people's faces, attitudes, and moods as they realize the show is yours. Who is glad and excited? Who is disappointed?

Now, you start reciting the lines of your monologue. You may hear a loud laugh exploding from a certain corner, just as you might get caught up in the reflection in someone's teared-up eyes... Notice this big audience's reaction and look for feedback, positive and negative, direct and indirect.

Tip - Research

Research could be a great idea, even if you and your thoughts are the product.

THE TARGET AUDIENCE

When selecting a target audience for a play, it's important to consider the production's content, theme, and style. Thus, to narrow down, identify, and pick a target audience, you first need to define your play's purpose, determining the goal or message of your play. Is it meant to entertain, educate, provoke thought, or evoke specific emotions?

Second, you need to analyze the content of your play, examining the subject matter, the language you choose to use, and the themes of your play. Is it age-appropriate? Is it complex? Does it involve any potentially sensitive or controversial topics?

Third, you may need to research the demographics of potential target audiences to understand their characteristics, such as age, gender, occupation, interests, cultural background, and socioeconomic status. Which groups might resonate most with the play's content and themes? Who would appreciate your message the most?

Finally, you may want to test the waters, gauging how different audiences may react to your message by gathering feedback and gauging their reactions.

Remember that the target audience may evolve, and it's essential to remain open to feedback and adjust your approach accordingly. Flexibility and adaptation are key when refining your understanding of your target audience for a play.

THE FRUIT MARKET

Before the harvest season, the wise and confident farmer searches for the appropriate markets where their product would fit well and be appreciated enough, hoping that their hard labor and tedious dedication would pay off. Similarly, after sharpening your character and rehearsing its embodiments time and time again, it's time for you to start searching for a good audience that would appreciate your show.

And just as the farmer ends up gathering a growing number of regular high-end customers by unfailingly providing the same quality of fruits, when the embodiment of your essence maintains its steadiness and consistency, you end up gathering an expanding pool of loyal audience, constituted of people who wait to hear your words, see your art, watch your inspirational videos on social media, or merely smile at your presence...

Fruitarians seeking the high nutritional benefits of premium-quality fruits might be among the farmer's top customers, along with reputable organic fruit purees and marmalade makers. Who are the people who need your nutrients, superpowers, and wisdom? Who are your people? Your target audience?

Some people, though, don't like fruits. Don't shove fruits down the throats of those who don't like them, and don't deny fruit lovers the fruits that you have. You don't sell fruits to someone needing basil to make pesto sauce.

Take the best pictures of their fruits, prepare a good monologue about their fruits and their quality, offer some fruits to be tasted as a sample... How will you advertise yourself?

PITCH YOUR PRODUCT

You have considered the Play's worldview and the values and guidelines that emerge from and support it, and you have accepted yourself as an irreplaceable character in the Play of Life. You have owned up to the central role of your own life play and become intimately acquainted with your irreplicable essence.

You took a closer look at your past and the depths of your being, then forged a stunning character profile, weaving together your backstory, traits, passions, aspirations, and superpowers. You embraced your unique authenticity and dedicated yourself to the faithful embodiment of your truth in all your great roles. You decluttered and optimized your environments to support and reflect you as well as possible. Then, you wrote down the next chapter of your life from this freshness.

Having developed a clear vision of where you're heading next, you handpicked the best backbone crew and supporting actors you could find, gathering a steadfast community of beautiful people who embrace you, uphold your journey, and strive to collaborate with you in your next life chapter.

Next, you rehearsed your lines and steps so often that they became second nature. Now, it is your time to share the fruits of your blood, sweat, and tears with the world. You have chosen your target audience carefully; now it is show time.

I no longer ask you to imagine, my dear Emiku. I now invite you to take action.

Pick a target audience, determine the date and place of your introduction of the new you to the world, and craft a thoughtful plan for revealing your new self.

Consider the various aspects of your life where you want to make the announcement—social media, personal meetings, or public events. Which channels are appropriate for promoting and marketing yourself and your message? They could be social media and online platforms, local publications, community centers, schools, or theaters frequented by your target audience.

Determine the message you wish to convey and the tone you want to set. Consider potential reactions and prepare yourself for different scenarios.

Tip - Authenticity

While you might doubt your excellence or feel pulled to borrow from others, trust yourself and remain faithful to your essence, vision, and mission. Nothing else matters.

- Date:

- Place:

- Target Audience:

- Outfit:

- Introductory Monologue: "Who am I?"

> *"I am devoted to my essence's honest and assertive advertisement."*

Chapter Ten
The Stage Is Yours
Rock it

As an artist, I always thought that the only legitimate stages were the ones existing in theaters designed by architects.

For several years, I tried to hide my authenticity and lived in the shadows, out of sight, to avoid conflicts and clashes. Little did I know that the entire world was a stage and everyone around me was part of an audience. It had never occurred to me that my only impermanent dear life was a play and that hiding behind the curtains was a deliberate choice of wasting it away in vain. For this reason, when I awakened at the shores of Lebanon, I recollected myself from the ashes like a phoenix and reclaimed my place under the spotlight in center stage!

Drumroll...

In this Act, sweet Emiku, it is my utmost pleasure and honor to give you ownership of your stage!

"Whichever way my feet wander, I will always stand center stage."

THREE MAGIC WORDS

As the director, you are the one having the authority to shout these three words:

Silence, Rolling, Action!

The silence before performing a role refers to the quiet contemplation and preparation an actor or performer engages in before going on stage or starting a scene. It is a moment of mental focus and concentration where the performer collects their thoughts, connect with their character, and prepare themselves emotionally and physically for the upcoming performance.

During this silence, performers may engage in various activities to get into the right mindset, such as deep breathing exercises, vocal warm-ups, stretching, or reviewing their lines or blocking. It is a time for self-reflection and channeling the energy necessary to embody the character they are about to portray fully.

The silence before performing a role serves several important purposes. It allows performers to center themselves, calm any nerves or anxiety, and enter a state of readiness. It also helps establish the necessary emotional and psychological space to immerse themselves fully in the character's world and the story.

Rolling, commonly known as "rolling the scene," is a term used to indicate the beginning of a scene or performance. A director, stage manager, or someone in charge often calls out rolling to cue the actors or performers to start their actions and dialogue.

In film and television productions, rolling refers to starting the camera recording. The director or the camera operator will typically call out "rolling" or "roll camera" to signal the camera crew to start recording. This is usually followed by the clapperboard being snapped shut to provide a visual and audio cue for synchronization during editing.

In theater, rolling can refer to initiating a scene or act. It signifies the moment when the lights, sound, and other technical elements are coordinated to signal the actors to begin their performance. It may also involve the movement of set pieces or changes in the stage environment to transition into the next scene.

Overall, rolling is a term used to indicate a scene's start, a camera's recording, or the commencement of a performance. It serves as a cue to synchronize the various elements of the production and guide the performers in their timing and execution.

Action on stage refers to actors' physical and verbal activities during a live performance. It encompasses various actions, including movement, dialogue, interactions with other characters, and executing specific tasks or scenes dictated by the script or performance requirements.

When actors take action on stage, they bring their characters to life through their physicality, vocal expression, and engagement with the other performers and the audience. This is the active and dynamic phase of performance where the narrative unfolds, conflicts arise, relationships are developed, and the story progresses.

The actions performed on stage include anything from simple movements like walking or sitting to complex choreography, fight sequences, or elaborate set changes. Each action is carefully planned and executed to convey the intended emotions, motivations, and storyline of the character and the overall production.

In summary, the silence before performing a role is the quiet period of mental preparation and focus that performers engage in before going on stage. On the other hand, action on stage refers to the active and dynamic physical and verbal activities performed by actors during the live performance. Both elements are integral to the theatrical experience and contribute to the overall success and impact of the performance.

UNDER THE SPOTLIGHT

Welcome to the final chapter, where the spotlight is yours. Today marks the beginning of a new chapter in your life, armed with the tools, resources, and wisdom from your past experiences and fueled by the vision of your future. It's time to bring your dreams to life. As this day unfolds, remember that it is your moment to show up for yourself, embrace the opportunity that lies before you, and shine.

Preparations have been made, and the stage is set. Just like the actors backstage, you enter three transformative mindsets. The first is disconnecting, where you let go of the outside world and fully immerse yourself in the character you aspire to be. Take a deep breath, meditate, and see yourself through your eyes, embracing your true essence in silence and stillness. Like a caterpillar evolving into a butterfly, you grow stronger and wiser, ready to overcome any challenges that come your way.

Today, you've sent out invitations to many, and the world is aware of your presence through advertisements. It's your grand performance; envision yourself backstage, awaiting a full audience. The stage is yours. The world needs inspiring, bold, courageous individuals who are unafraid to be themselves.

The world eagerly awaits your powerful embodiment of who you are. As you step into the spotlight, let your authentic expression reign.

To initiate change in your life journey, start by transforming your inner world. Enter the backstage of your mind, quieting the chatter and embracing your authentic self. The more you rehearse, the more the script becomes part of who you are, becoming the character you wish to play.

Silence!

After the silence, as your mind settles, you tap into the realm of embodying your knowing, transcending mere knowledge. The curtains remain closed, and then comes the moment to roll into action.

Rolling!

Now, you are fully prepared. Inhale deeply, don your crown, and show up.

Action!

The third mindset is action. Stepping onto the stage, the curtain lifts, centering the spotlight on you. With confidence, you unveil your true self.

THE END

As the final notes of the symphony fade into the ether, the audience stands and applauds you. The theater starts to empty, leaving you alone on the vast stage. The spotlight's glow wanes, casting shadows that gently embrace the edges of the auditorium. One by one, the lights dim, like stars surrendering to the night's embrace.

A smile of contentment graces your lips in the peaceful stillness, for you have forged a stubborn connection with the soul-stirring artistry that resides within you. The applause echoes reverberate through the hollow expanse, growing softer yet sweeter with each passing moment.

The last few people leave. The purple curtains close. You're left alone just behind them. With a tender touch, your palms unite, creating a cadence that resonates with gratitude. In this solitary act of self-celebration, you honor the countless hours of practice, the unwavering commitment, and your belief in your brilliance. You feel drops of cold, refreshing blood passing through your heart and getting pumped again towards the extremity of every limb. It's electrical, and you feel alive like never before.

In the dimming theater, the echoes of your applause intertwine with the whispers of the night, reminding you that the audience does not bind your journey. In this moment, you stand as an actor, director, and spectator, acknowledging the power of your own applause and the profound significance of your passion.

Imagine all the people you want to be watching you sitting in the audience. I smile to you...And as I clap for you, the faces of the people you imagined to be here start fading one by one. There's only the two of us left here.

I stand up, giving you the ovation you deserve. I bow down in reverence to your essence and this exquisite embodiment. You can sense my deep appreciation and pride. I start walking away and smile at you one last time as I cross the thick wooden doors of the house. They close behind me.

You're alone.

THE BEGINNING

You feel deeply moved as you stand alone in this big theater, in the place of the strange woman who invited you on this journey. And what a journey it was. Whether it felt heavy or light, intense or a play in the park, it was what it was, and thus, it was perfect.

The different pitstops of the journey roll before you... You have learned all the techniques; the stage is yours, life is a long journey, rehearse as much as you need, review and advertise yourself in new communities, and go on new adventures and new territories. Be prepared for the exciting journey ahead. Remember who you would've still been today hadn't you changed and remained confined. You're the life director and scriptwriter; you rehearsed it, and it's time to break free and soar.

May you always be your own greatest backbone, your most loyal, unwavering fan. Embrace self-belief, stand up for yourself, take action, and be. Unleash your unwavering spirit and authenticity as you embark on your extraordinary path, captivating the world with your brilliance and enchantment. Embrace the uniqueness within you, illuminating the realms of possibility and crafting a destiny unlike any other. Let your journey be a symphony of dreams and aspirations, inspiring all who witness your remarkable presence.

This journey invites you to embrace your true self and courageously applaud yourself when no one's around.

You clap for yourself.

"The Stage is Mine!"

After "The Stage is Yours"

IN THIS BOOK, I give you a testimonial of my journey and how I transformed each situation into a learning experience and put it into a plan for my future.

Being the actor, director, producer, and scriptwriter might sound like a lot of roles. That's why I created this method: to help us dig deeper into our beliefs and find the essence of who we are by putting all our learnings into action.

I created "the Life Director Coaching Method' course, which you can find online on my website, www.thelifedirector.com. In this course, we dig into our belief system and how we create every situation. We will learn how to reprogram our subconscious mind to support our conscious vision so we can overcome all the challenges we might face along the way as we break the negative patterns that no longer serve us. Then, most importantly, we will learn how to heal our wounds and forgive ourselves and the people involved in our stories so we can move forward with love and peace. By completing the course, you would become certified as a Life Director.

I also put together "the Life Director Retreat," where I will work with you in person to help you create your script, put your life into practice, and act your life in front of your eyes using real actors while you sit in the director's chair, owning your vision and directing your life the way you planned it.

Review Request

Thank you so much for reading this book. I realize millions of books are out there, and I want to express my infinite appreciation for your choosing mine.

Now that you have finished reading this book, it would be a huge favor to me and future readers if you left feedback on Amazon.

If you enjoyed this book (and I think you did if you got to the end), please leave a review—this is one of the only ways authors like myself can find readers like you.

If you wish to write a review (and I hope you do), you can do that in any of the following three ways:

Visit the Amazon review page of this book:

https://www.amazon.com/Stage-Yours-Motivational-Discovering
-Manifesting/dp/1965480187

Acknowledgements

Moustafa Hamwi: The one who insisted and pushed me hard to get this book out from day one.

Serge: My husband, who never gave up on me throughout my journey and did his best to embrace and hold me.

Laeticia and Nicolas: My kids, whose excitement kept me going and whose pride in me kept me fueled.

My late parents: They were the ones who gave me so much love and helped me spread my wings again.

My siblings: They kept on boosting my confidence, reminding me of who I was in times of pain and sadness.

My close friends: The ones whose valuable input was so indispensable for the writing of the book.

Caroline: My late friend, the one who knew me very well. I can't express how much I wish you were here. Be certain that a part of you lives in every chapter.

Nayritta: My soul sister, the one who mirrors me the most. Thank you for your patience and presence.

Dalia: The one who supported and fortified each and every step I took. I'm grateful for our magical encounters. Thank you for believing in me.

Marcelino: The one who held for me, who allowed me to bring what was on my mind to reality.

Carine: The one who comforted me when I wanted to take a break. I'm grateful for all of our walks on the beach. Each one meant the world to me.

Farah and Georges: They helped me edit the book in such a short time.

God: The one who's been my life director all along.

About Nadine Chammas

Growing up in Lebanon, Nadine pursued her passion for singing and theater, specializing in Dramatics and Theatre Arts. This led to a successful career in acting, producing, and directing plays. In Dubai, she founded *Scenez Group Production Company*, crafting culture-bridging shows for major events, like *the Dubai Shopping Festival* and *Dubai Summer Surprises,* to name a few. Later, Nadine established *Scenez Drama and Arts Academy in DUCTAC*, offering drama therapy for children and adults.

As a mother, she connected with others through counseling sessions on Al Arabiya and set up the *Super Dooper Edutainment Center* for children's learning.

Nadine's continuous pursuit of knowledge includes certifications in NLP Coaching, Positive Parenting, Life Coaching, Transformational Therapy, and Stage Hypnosis, making her the first female stage hypnotist in the Middle East. Combining her experiences, she embraced the power of positivity. She committed to building awareness and spreading joy, leading her to create an online program for the regional professional growth platform *Al Mentor*. She founded **"The**

Life Director," a consultancy firm specializing in positive lifestyle programs.

Alongside her professional accomplishments, Nadine's music has resonated with millions during the COVID-19 pandemic, with over 1.2 million views on YouTube. She remains an inspiring figure, delivering motivational talks and empowering individuals and organizations through her diverse expertise and insights.

Connect with Nadine on www.thelifedirector.com